A Hobby Out of Control

MAR '07

DEB —
YOU MUST REVIEW
YOUR DAD — HE SAID
HE MUST HAVE THE BOOK —
$ MOST
NOTICE THE MOST
Bill

A Hobby Out of Control

Ten Life-Based Lessons for Young Entrepreneurs

William "Bill" Locklin,
founder, Nightscaping™

Copyright © 2007 by William "Bill" Locklin.

ISBN 10:	Hardcover	1-4257-4376-5
	Softcover	1-4257-4375-7
ISBN 13:	Hardcover	978-1-4257-4376-5
	Softcover	978-1-4257-4375-8

All rights reserved. No part of this book may be reproduced or transmitted in any form or by any means, electronic or mechanical, including photocopying, recording, or by any information storage and retrieval system, without permission in writing from the copyright owner.

This book was printed in the United States of America.

To order additional copies of this book, contact:
Xlibris Corporation
1-888-795-4274
www.Xlibris.com
Orders@Xlibris.com

Contents

Preface 9

Introduction 11

Chapter 1—Believe in Yourself 15
    My Story 15
    Concepts 22
    10 Reflection Questions 23

Chapter 2—Be Resourceful . . . and Persistent 24
    My Story 24
    Concepts 32
    10 Reflection Questions 33

Chapter 3—Follow Your Instincts . . . . and Interests 34
    My Story 34
    Concepts 39
    10 Reflection Questions 40

Chapter 4—Search for Knowledge 41
    My Story 41
    Concepts 50
    10 Reflection Questions 51

Chapter 5—Success Is *Mañana* 52
    My Story 52
    Concepts 60
    10 Reflection Questions 61

Chapter 6—Make Friends . . . . a Lot of Friends 62
    My Story 62
    Concepts 70
    10 Reflection Questions 71

Chapter 7—Get Involved in Your Local (and Non-Local) Communities........72
    My Story 72
    Concepts..78
    10 Reflection Questions...79

Chapter 8—Understand Your Customers' Motivations 80
    My Story 80
    Concepts..87
    10 Reflection Questions...88

Chapter 9—Watch Out for Professional Advice
(and Conventional Wisdom)...89
    My Story 89
    Concepts..98
    10 Reflection Questions...99

Chapter 10—Manage Fairly (Groom Your Employees to Be Great)............100
    My Story 100
    Concepts..107
    10 Reflection Questions...108

The 10 Most Important Reminders..109

Friends Doing Business with Friends...111

*To the young entrepreneurs that might read about,
and benefit from, these experiences.*

Preface

It's about time that a man who could take a tomato juice can and a tractor headlight bulb and build them into a multimillion-dollar business shared some of his business knowledge with others. This can-and-bulb contraption was the first fixture Bill Locklin used as he was inventing low-voltage landscape lighting. No one else had the foresight to come up with something as simple as this, which turned the landscape industry from high voltage to low-voltage lighting. It was his knowledge of lighting that started the industry we have today.

Ever since Bill hired his first employee, a phone call to the Nightscaping plant—"May I speak to Bill please"—has been answered a few seconds later with "This is Bill." He is a rarity in today's business world: no secretary, no voicemail, just Bill Locklin. He's always been supportive of his distributors and installation contractors and is always available to speak personally to you. His personal touch in dealing with the day-to-day workings of his company is truly unique.

A book from Bill has been needed for a long time. Over the past 45-plus years, I have personally "stolen" many business ideas from him—such as having educational classes, one of which was the "Nightscaping University®" for his distributors and their contractors. This led directly to my company presenting a yearly "Super Bowl of Lighting" to educate our contractors. Bill has always been supportive of my company, both monetarily and by imparting ideas. I give "the Man in Levi's" as much credit for the success of our company as I could give anyone who doesn't work here every day.

I wish him well in this new endeavor. He is certainly well qualified to set forth his ideas in a volume such as this.

Dave McWilliams
President/CEO
Calif. Landscape Lighting

Introduction

To kick off this introduction, I'll introduce myself.

My name is Bill Locklin. I'm the inventor of 12-volt outdoor lighting and the founder of Nightscaping, a company I've run for more than 40 years. My business began with a fortuitous meeting with a United States president, has run through numerous calamities and technical/societal changes, and continues to survive and thrive today.

Nightscaping complex and staff

Welcome to the story of my life and career. So far they've both been very good, and for that I am thankful. And that's why I'm writing this book.

At the typing of this page, I'm an 85-year-old man. I've learned a lot from my experiences. Now I want to share them. I hope what they teach about entrepreneurship and business success will help those just starting out on their own. Help them make their careers everything they want them to be. I believe it will.

What am I trying to accomplish with this book? Two very simple things.

First, I want to relate to you some of the key episodes of my working life in an interesting and entertaining way. Second, I want to highlight the lessons these episodes have taught me.

This has led me to a very simple structure for this book. First I talk about the idea in general terms, explaining how it's helped my business and why I think it's important. Each of my ten lessons is illustrated with a few incidents from my life. After that I formulate the key concepts in easy-to-understand, bulleted fashion. Finally I provide a series of questions at the end of each chapter that encourage the reader to explore related ideas in more depth.

Each chapter in this book is a lesson—and each lesson is plainly stated in the title. It's never that easy, however, to learn something. Wouldn't it be great if we could just hear a maxim like "Be Resourceful" or "Get Involved Locally" and understand exactly what it meant, and why we should follow this advice? Of course it would.

Unfortunately, I've found people don't work like that. Everyone has to learn, and relearn, even the most common truths for themselves. And it's rare that you hear a teaching, or piece of advice, and assimilate it—really own it—without testing it in your own reality. In your own experience of the world.

So why try to teach at all? Why not just let people learn the basic truths on their own? Well, people have to stumble across them on their own. True.

But when you're lost and find a new place, it helps if you have a map. Something to match the new place up with. This makes it much easier to remember how to return.

Stories can help with this, of course. One of the traditional reasons people tell stories is to pass on knowledge and information. Though I don't expect mine will enable you, right away, to start a successful business, I do think they'll serve as helpful signposts when you've stumbled off the worn path, and, perhaps, are on the verge of discovering a whole set of wonderful new ideas.

As I developed my business I made a lot of good friends—an important concept in its own right and one we'll talk more about later. I never, however, had someone there the entire time, showing me the ropes, telling me how things work.

Most entrepreneurs don't. Instead they follow their own ideas, their own instructions. It's a dangerous route, but usually, unless you're very lucky, it's the only way to go about it. And even if you do have someone there, a mentor of sorts, advice can take you only so far. Your situations, needs, and dilemmas will often be unique to you, and the words of others won't necessarily apply.

If you have sound fundamentals, however, if you understand the bedrock of successful business practices, you will have signposts to guide you. It's these fundamentals—the ones I've found most useful, anyway—that I wish to explain.

Though my business is a technical one, involving outdoor lighting and based on innovations I pioneered more than 45 years ago, I believe my story has universal lessons that will benefit anyone striking out on their own in a commercial world. Why?

- Every new business, the vast, vast majority of them, anyway, revolve around sales. A service or goods provided. Most have customers or clients.

- Every new business requires resourcefulness and tenacity, in addition to a strong inner reservoir of strength and confidence in your ability to succeed.

- Every new business requires both knowledge and good personal relationships. The latter applies both to those inside the business, between the business and clients or customers, and between the business and other businesses.

- Most lasting businesses require a local anchor, a healthy tie to the community or communities in which it's based.

- Every new business requires a thorough understanding of client needs.

- Every new business requires a great deal of hard work in the beginning—a long-view focus on tomorrow, and the day after tomorrow.

So while of course this book will be of extra interest to those wanting to get into the commercial lighting business, or technical innovators of any sort, it's intended to serve a general audience as well, providing lessons applicable to anyone beginning a new company. These are very important people in terms of the American economy, and they are some of the best and the brightest our country has to offer. I wish to do all I can to help.

I believe deeply in America and the strength that comes from American small businesses. I believe that with hard work, sacrifice, and gumption, anyone can make it here, regardless of race, religion, etc. Why do I believe this?

My own early years were difficult.

I was born in Alhambra, California, 1921. Shortly thereafter I was abandoned in a train station in Victorville. So I became, and remained, an orphan. I grew up a ward of the county of San Bernardino.

My adolescent years weren't particularly impressive or beautiful. I spent more time in detention centers than school. I dropped out of high school.

In other words, I wasn't exactly on what you would call the path to success.

The fact that I'm still around, running a business more than 60 years later, should go to show you—if you didn't already know—that in this country, anything can happen. I came from zero, basically, and worked that into the five-acre, eight-building complex from which I now run my company, Nightscaping®.

It didn't happen overnight, though. That's one cliché you should fully believe. I know movies and TVs are plastered with people who (supposedly) got rich or became successful overnight. And then lived happily ever after.

Doesn't work like that, as far as I've ever seen.

For most people, a real lifelong success is years, decades, in the building. It requires long nights, a sacrifice of "what everyone else has," and a tenacious clinging to the vision in your mind. What it doesn't require, however, is some special genius.

The quote from Albert Einstein, "Genius is one percent inspiration and ninety-nine percent perspiration," I've found to be just about right. I had an inspiration over forty years ago concerning outdoor lighting, and I've been fighting ever since to build and maintain a business centered around it.

Did I wake up one morning and suddenly have this tremendous vision? No. My innovation was based on years of slow knowledge accruement and practical experience. It may not be glamorous or made-for-TV, but in my long lifetime I've found this experience is far more common among successful entrepreneurs than is the "lightning-bolt" type. Remember, lightning bolts only light up the sky for a moment.

You want to be more like the sun. Difficult enough.

So take heart. While this book, the culmination of sixty-five years and more spent in my field, won't turn you into a millionaire overnight, or magically grow/fix a business without any effort from you, it should give you some conception of the pillars of good business practice.

I wasn't born with this knowledge. Being an electrician first and businessman second, I had to learn, feel, my way through the minefield of entrepreneurship.

This is the map I came back with. I hope you find it instructive.

Chapter 1

Believe in Yourself

My Story

A lot of young people today wonder what it takes to be a successful businessperson. More specifically, they want to know if there's a constant, an underlying formula. Maybe some factor of birth or upbringing that allows a person to succeed—that guarantees he will. They look at a successful person and wonder what lies at the core—what separates this one from all the others who've not made it.

There's a downside to this state of mind. All too often young people—or even those who aren't so young—become convinced there certainly is a special quality, and while they don't know what exactly it is, they come to believe they lack it. This belief can hurt potential entrepreneurs in several ways. First, it can prevent them from getting off the ground in the first place. The idea that you can't make a boat float is the hardest thing to shake, but it must be shaken if you're ever to set off on your own. Second, the idea that you lack a certain something can prove corrosive, leading you to sabotage your own best efforts and ultimately making your perceived, mysterious fault into a self-fulfilling prophecy. But it isn't true.

Remember Franklin Roosevelt. Remember that fear is the only thing of which we have to be afraid. Young people must know, cannot survive in business without knowing, that there's nothing separating the successful from the unsuccessful but hard work, common sense, and persistence. Doesn't luck come into it? Of course, but it's a matter of degree. Luck may turn your $2 million business into a $5 million business, but it won't turn your ideas into a strategy, or turn your struggling business into a sound one.

In other words, luck is the residue of design, as another famous quote goes. You've seen those overnight successes on TV? The ones who designed a widget that just so happened to become Widget-of-the-Month, and thus never had to work another day in their lives? Forget them. They're as rare as lottery winners. In fact that's exactly what they are—their ticket was starting a business, and they beat the longest odds. For 99.9% of small-business owners, this kind of luck will never appear. So forget about luck, forget about getting rich quick, and focus on the long term.

Forgetting about luck will help you separate out the "mystery" of success. The mystery is why anyone thinks it's still a mystery. The only secret is that there isn't one. Your chance is as good as anyone else's—you can go as high as your work capacity, desire, and natural abilities take you. There are no chosen ones, no predetermined successes.

For those who aren't convinced, I offer the beginning of my own life as an example.

Far from being a "golden child," I was left in a train depot at the age of three weeks. I'd been born on June 25th at the Los Angeles County Hospital in Alhambra. Twenty-odd days after emerging into the world, I was left alone in it.

Except I wasn't. The Victorville station master found me and carried me across the tracks to the Summers Inn, run by Charles and Kate Summers. They were in their fifties, childless, and the kicking and squirming newborn (me) in the station master's charge quickly stole their hearts.

They decided to adopt me. Problem was, I had no papers. Thus I was placed in their home as a ward of San Bernardino County.

A few months later, the cowboy actor Tom Mix came to film a movie in Victorville and stayed at the Summers Inn. Though the silent-film actor married seven times (to six women), I suppose he still had room for a child, because he, too, wanted to adopt me. Again the problem of my undocumented status reared its ugly head, and Mr. Mix rode off into the sunset without me.

I grew up in the Summers Inn, which was eventually shuttered when Charles and Kate decided to move to Lucerne Valley and start raising alfalfa. Charles's farming roots ran deep, and I suppose they'd both tired of keeping house for others. Back on the land, I guess they did alright. For a while, at least.

My formal education began in a one-room, grades 1-8 schoolhouse. I made it only a few days before being sent home. Why? I put a garter snake in the teacher's desk. She never did see the real reason for this.

I had a few friends. One of the first was the daughter of our closest neighbors. When the miners turned their burros loose in the summer, all of us kids would claim one to ride and generally harass until fall. This girl and I chose one and shared it, with her riding face forward on the beast and me facing the rear.

Quite a romance.

We had precious few other entertainments. She was the artist in our neighborhood, she was quite artistic. She would make lifelike cardboard cutouts of barnyard animals and fences and whatnot, so that we could have entire farms right there on the ground. In the 1920s this was considered big fun.

Later on this young lady left the farm and became one of Walt Disney's early artists.

Life was okay. Then came the stock market crash of 1929. The price of alfalfa fell to a hair north of zero. The Summers lost their farm and moved to Hemet, a town in the middle of the dry zone between Los Angeles and Palm Springs.

As you can see, my upbringing was less than storybook. I had the good fortune of living with decent people, true, but I certainly was never marked for success. At this point I was just a boy trying to survive. And that never changed much.

I did eventually meet my father. He found me in Hemet somehow and took me to Denver to meet my mother. I remember very little of the trip, as I was still a small boy. The only thing that truly sticks out in my memory is that it seemed as if we had a flat tire every ten miles or so. In Denver things were even less memorable. All I can say is that it wasn't a situation of which a youngster would dream.

Soon I returned to Hemet and the Summers. The only problem was the Summers were aging fast. Now in their 60s, they were too tired to continue raising me. Especially since I was a rebellious boy. And an unhappy one.

Once again I became a ward of the county.

I spent plenty of time in a detention center, as I was becoming nearly impossible to control. Eventually I was placed in a foster home. A good, strict Christian home.

I don't have many fond memories from this period of my life, either. There wasn't much happening for me early on. So I often tried to make things happen.

For instance, this couple with whom I lived had a much older son who was stricken by polio, terribly disabled, and wheelchair bound. He and I were friends. One day we decided to make some wine. I don't know why, we just thought to do it.

I rode my bicycle out to the vineyards and snipped enough grapes to make some grape juice at home. We had a gallon left over for the wine. Into a jug we poured the juice. We'd seen or heard somewhere that you had to cork it, then fasten down the cork with string. We did this, then left the jug down in a corner of the basement to make wine.

A while later, on Christmas Eve, we went into the basement to retrieve our wine. We dug the jug out of its hiding place. To my surprise the deep red juice was now clear, with a bit of sediment on the bottom. Great! Let's try it.

First we had to cut the string holding down the cork, however. I set the jug on my buddy's lap and took out my pocket knife. Didn't take much.

I'd barely touched the blade to the string when the fermented juice exploded out of the bottle, rocketing up to the ceiling, then down all over us. Drenching us in the very sour smelling "wine." Wasn't much chance of covering it up, either, with my buddy in the wheelchair. So it wasn't a very merry Christmas, in the end.

Thus went most of my childhood.

However, I don't want you to get the idea that I'm sour on life. I'm not trying to plead hardship or draw your sympathy, either. I am truly fortunate in all the wonderful breaks that have come my way in life. I believe life is a balance; what you get shorted on at one point, you generally get back at another.

I've included this material to show that not everyone who builds a successful business comes out of some privileged background. Or has some special aura surrounding them during their childhood. If you asked me I'd say I was an average boy.

So what made the difference? Believing in myself—and my ability to learn, then do, something. Anything. This is what's gotten me to where I am today.

Though this trait can get you into trouble as a businessperson (sometimes you'll bite off more than you can chew), there's almost no way to get along without it.

When I returned from World War II, from nearly five years riding around on submarines in the Pacific Theater, I had the rank of chief electrician's mate. What else did I have? A young wife and daughter. But what could I do?

Submarine crew (me with bald dome)

Well, first I got a job as an electrician's helper at the local cement company.

While I was trying to figure out the rest I took the California license exam for electrical contractors. Passed that, and right away I contracted with Southern California Edison. It was 1945, the beginning of tract houses. My job was to convert wired meter boxes to three-wired (because everyone now needed a clothes dryer) for $33 a house. My contract was for ten houses.

The total contract, parts and labor, came to about $400. This was my first real independent job. Had I ever wired a house? Nope.

And I never could have taken this step if I wasn't confident in my ability to learn to do it, and do it right. *As long as someone can do it, I can do it.* That's a good way to look at aspects of a job you have no experience with. All you have to do is make sure it doesn't take skills or equipment you don't have (and can't acquire before the deadline).

My first move was to go to other tracts and see how contractors were wiring them. After a few days of figuring it out, I began. Soon I had the houses wired.

They're still standing, with lights on, to this day.

A few years later, after I was a more established electrician, with a much wider range of experiences, I again found myself in a job that required knowledge I didn't have.

The Redlands Bowl, in my current home of Redlands, California, is the site of the oldest free music festival in the United States. Every summer, on starry, balmy nights, up to six thousand people fill its outdoor benches and lawn to hear various types of music, from jazz to classical to opera to bluegrass. The stage lighting for the theater was done, when I first moved to Redlands, by an old-timer who'd actually done the original wiring for the place back in the 1920s.

Redlands bowl

This old-timer, the town's established electrical contractor, told me shortly after I arrived that he was retiring after 15 years of running stage lights. Guess who he chose as his replacement? That's right. The new kid.

So I went down to inspect the premises. My new field of play. What did I find? An endless array of cables, patch cords, dimmer switches, lighting gels, and who knows what else. I was blown away. I'd mastered the wiring on a submarine, I'd worked on enormous industrial jobs, but running the lights for a mid-sized regional theater seemed far beyond my scope.

The old-timer assured me I'd pick it all up in no time. Still, the only one who could really convince me of that fact was . . . me. And it wasn't easy.

My predecessor left me to my own devices quickly, without much training to speak of. And that's how I found myself, one hot summer evening, preparing lighting for a visiting San Francisco ballet troupe. With no idea of what I was doing.

Which colors do I use? I had no idea. In fact, all the various gels and colored lights had been my biggest concern. How do you pick between red and blue?

Some words of the old-timer came back to me. "If they don't have a stage manager, go backstage and see what the predominant costume colors are. Your lights need to complement them."

Complement them? I'm a simple electrician. And at this point in my career, when I was being shown how to do things, I often nodded without fully understanding. *Compliment?* What the heck do colors have to say nice to each other?

I went backstage as my mentor suggested. All I see are pink tutus. They're lining the room. They're everywhere. So, naturally, I knew I needed a lot of pink light. Right up I went, putting pink gels all over the light trees.

Now the patron saint of the Redlands Bowl and its festival was a woman who would sit all the way in the back, behind the 5000 or so people who'd come to watch her show. Back there with her she kept a telephone that connected directly to my little control room. Just in case something was a bit off.

The Redlands Bowl had no curtains to raise. So the custom was to bring all the lights up just as it got dark, on a downbeat from the orchestra. Well, that evening I cue up my lights, the starting time comes, the orchestra gives the signal, and let 'em rip.

The first thing I hear is a giant AHH . . . HAHA from what seemed like the entire audience at once. The next thing I hear is the patron saint screaming in my ear.

"The lights! The lights! It looks like the dancers don't have any clothes on!"

Oops. Pink light, for the record, does not complement pink clothing. In fact, it tends to make it disappear. My mistake.

I recovered from it, however, and over the next 15 years, I ran the lights at the Redlands Bowl every Tuesday and Friday night in the summer. And, believe me, I learned all about outdoor color lighting. I even learned what *complement* meant, in regards to colors.

All this is simply to say that had I not believed in myself, had I been unwilling, or too scared, to make the inevitable mistake, I never would have gotten this very fun and very rewarding job. In fact I probably never would have made the innovations I did or begin Nightscaping, because it was my experience with outdoor theatrical lighting that made me dissatisfied with the quality of available 120-volt landscape options.

So, by picking up a job for which I was definitely unqualified, by believing that I could do what the man before me—an electrical contractor just like me—had done, I opened up a whole new world, of which I'd been completely ignorant. This knowledge not only made me a more competent electrician in general, expanding my skills, it also opened the door to what would become a lifelong career.

After all, my job at Nightscaping is to show houses off to their best advantage, just as I did for singers and dancers many years ago in the Redlands Bowl. But what if I'd been too afraid of making a mistake to accept the job. What if I'd thought, *No—I'll leave this to someone who's better than me. I should stick to what I know.*

I don't know what. I probably would have stuck to wiring houses, wind machines, and deep-well pumps rather than beginning a business I've nurtured (and loved) for more than forty years. But I was ready to grow and learn. Expand my field of play.

The same goes for the job wiring houses in 1945. I'd never done that before. I surely could have avoided it, avoided the risk that's always there when you try new things, when you stretch yourself out. I surely could have gotten my old job at the cement factory back and spent the rest of my life working for someone else, dealing with the specific industrial controls facing me every day, and then retiring without ever learning anything else. Could have been like that.

But no, I wanted to push myself and learn all I could. I was open to doing new tasks, experimenting with my skills and acquiring new ones.

Anyone who wants to become a successful entrepreneur must be willing to learn a wide, wide range of new skills. Perhaps you'll find yourself working with things you never thought you would—a computer, a camera, a delivery van . . . maybe even a mop. You never know what you'll have to do. So you learn how to do everything you can.

And believe, at each step, that you can do it well.

Concepts

- **Fear** holds back a large number of would-be entrepreneurs.

- Many young people who would like to start their own businesses, or simply strive for high-level roles in their working lives, believe they **lack something essential** to do so, or, similarly, that successful people are **somehow born with something special** that allows them to succeed.

- This kind of outlook will often lead people to become **afraid of success** and sabotage their own best efforts. After all (they think), they're not supposed to succeed, right? So if they do, something will be wrong with the universe.

- There is **no magic formula** that assures a person of success in business or life. Determination is probably the biggest indicator of who will prevail in their entrepreneurship.

- In fact, what separates successful entrepreneurs from others is a **strong work ethic** and an unfailing **belief in themselves.** (Of course, fantastic wealth and great connections help, too, but I assume people with these advantages won't need the services of my book.)

- Part of believing in yourself is **having faith in your ability to learn new skills** and **master new concepts.** Any entrepreneur or small-businessperson necessarily needs to become proficient in a wide range of varied skills—jobs that would normally be the niche of a number of people in a large business automatically fall to the proprietor of smaller start-ups.

- **Saying yes** to opportunities offered to you or your business, even if they require some stretching out, some learning, and perhaps some failure, is the only way to succeed and grow.

- As a wise man once said, **a success is merely a failure who keeps getting up.** The point is that not only is failure expected, it is almost mandatory for people who hope to accomplish anything in life.

- Is there risk involved in **saying yes** and growing? Of course there is. Any time you stretch yourself, you're moving out of your comfort zone and inviting some kind of disturbance. The key, however, is to expect and welcome the disturbance. You'll never grow without it.

10 Reflection Questions

The following questions are not fill-in-the-blank-type questions. Instead, they're meant to spark you, to get you thinking about things we tend not to deal with on a daily basis. For anyone who's reexamining their life or looking for something more, these questions will hopefully provide some starting points for a new career path.

1. What is it that you most want to accomplish?

2. What's the single greatest obstacle, in your opinion, holding you back from that accomplishment?

3. How big a role does fear play in your thought process? Do you tend to get nervous or anxious when you succeed in front of others, or are put in positions of responsibility?

4. If yes, where do you believe this fear comes from?

5. What could be the worst possible outcome of your success? And of your failure?

6. In a work situation are you one of the first to volunteer yourself for new challenges? If not, why?

7. How well do you handle defeat? Are you easily discouraged? Do you give up quickly? In what type of activities are you more persistent? Why?

8. Do you tend to stick with familiar skill sets, or are you open to acquiring new ones? How quickly do you adapt to, and integrate, new knowledge?

9. Do you regularly identify and explore new opportunities?

10. Think of five reasons you can succeed as a small business owner, then think of five reasons you can't. Which list is easier to come up with? Which is stronger?

Chapter 2

Be Resourceful . . . and Persistent

My Story

At the end of World War II, we were living in Colton, California—just east of Los Angeles and south of Victorville (where, for me, it all began). I'd just begun my career as an electrical contractor. I also had two little girls and a wife in a small home. Space was at a premium. *Boy*, I thought, *it would be nice to have a little area to work with.*

I was in luck. At that time the US government was selling a great deal of its surplus equipment from the war. One such item was the Quonset hut—the semicircular lightweight steel sheds made famous in the Pacific Theater.

Our submarine battle flag

These structures were easy to move and assemble, provided nearly a 1,000 square feet of work space, and, most importantly, were available for a song.

The government had purchased around 165,000 Quonset huts during the war. Now they were offering them to the public for $1,000 or less. A good bargain for a complete and durable structure. So I bought one, set it up on a leased lot in Colton.

The back of the hut became my workshop and construction headquarters. The front part I glassed in and made into a small retail shop for electrical items. I kept the store open from seven to eight in the morning and from five to six thirty at night. In between I would wire tract houses and perform other such jobs.

Though I had at this time no inkling of my future product or how my business would evolve, this hut provided me with a beginning—gave me the space I needed to evolve. This is extremely important. Eventually this hut would host the seeds of my current company, Nightscaping.

It's essential that, as an entrepreneur, you have a place dedicated to your work. It doesn't matter if you're a writer, bicycle repairman, or a singer. You'll need some place to build, practice, fix, or imagine. A bedroom, living room, or kitchen table can only take you so far. The practical advantages of having a personal space are innumerable. Yet there's also an important psychological boost that comes from having your own "office." It lends legitimacy to your pursuit, both in the eyes of others and in your own mind. I find this highly important, as often one of the biggest mental obstacles in starting your own business will be convincing yourself, deeply and completely, of the seriousness of your pursuit.

I still monkey around at my "destruct" bench

A novelist named Virginia Woolf once said a person needs "a room of one's own" to write full time. (She also advised an income of 500 pounds sterling a year—an inheritance for her, but something I, and most reading this book, needed to sweat for.) Far from only applying to writers, I think this serves anyone who wants to create something new (any entrepreneur is necessarily creative).

I had my cheap Quonset hut. Sadly, they're not available anymore, but there are opportunities. Seek out space in buildings, or parts of town, that look a little down at the heel. Chances are you'll find a landlord willing to make a few dollars on his unused space. The key here is to be resourceful. This country (and the world) is full of things unused, whether we're talking about floor space, equipment, or materials. You'll be amazed what you can find, once you know what you're looking for (and where to look).

When starting a new business, it's very helpful to become a scavenger of sorts. Don't be afraid to gather what someone else spills. Keeping your initial costs low while acquiring things that advance your business—this is a time-tested ingredient of success.

On the other hand, if you're not resourceful, if you either acquire everything at cost, through traditional retail channels, or go without, you'll have much less chance for success. You must begin to see what the universe is offering you, to take advantage of the things life is putting right in front of you. This is an essential aspect of the entrepreneurial spirit.

I learned more than one important lessons in this during the immediate postwar years, three of which I spent traveling the United States with my wife and daughters. One episode that has remained vividly with me occurred on a highway bridge outside Birmingham, Alabama, to which I was traveling for work.

Now in those days you would still see horses in quite a few towns and cities, and people weren't always as smart and efficient about some things concerning roads and construction. As was the case on this particular occasion.

A survey crew had set up their equipment in the middle of this bridge, stopping traffic completely in both directions. Being from California, used to whizzing around and always being in a hurry, I began fuming and fussing, angry that this crew hadn't the brains to set up on one side of the road or other, thus leaving a lane for passing.

As I was griping at the wheel of my car, another gentleman behind me pulled up and got out to inspect the situation. After taking in the survey crew and realizing we weren't going to move for a while, the man promptly returned to his car. There he took off his tie, rolled up his sleeves, and opened the trunk. From which he removed a fishing pole.

While the rest of us sat and steamed, this guy caught a beautiful mess of bass for supper. Thinking about this in the many years since then, I've realized that his actions had a profound impact on me. It was the beginning of a set of lessons that would teach me more than just how to be a good or successful electrician. It was indeed an answer, in some part, to life. This lesson in resourcefulness, in utilizing the best of what's available to you in a given moment, translated well into my business life, too.

Resourcefulness is also a matter of deciding what's important and what's not. Of realizing what materials and equipment are essential, and which ones are simply the customary window dressing. No one starts up with unlimited funds. So it's very helpful to cut out of your operation everything that's going to weigh it down with unwieldy overhead or capital expenditure.

Many major businesses are currently subscribing to the same approach. Look at budget airlines like Jet Blue or Southwest—the no-frills approach is the only profitable way to run an airline these days. Look at Google, whose multibillion-dollar search engine was, and still is, fronted by the simplest webpage you can imagine, with its only graphics the logo and no more than a dozen or so words on it at any given time. Stripped-down is the new watchword in business, and what works for the big buys (in this case) will work double for you. The trick is to focus on what you do, and focus like a laser, acquiring just enough to invent, modify, and perfect your goods or services.

The other side of this: base your business on your strengths, not on what you *think* you should be doing. Let me give you another example based on my life.

After our three years on the road we returned to San Bernardino—more specifically, my current home of Redlands, California. It was here that I began getting jobs installing outdoor lighting for private homes. At first I used regular 120-volt fixtures, though the selection for outdoor lighting was slim. I was dissatisfied with the aesthetic effects produced by 120V (obviously, my theatrical work was already having an impact on the way I perceived things).

So I began working with a 12-volt current. This was the current generated by car batteries, and I found it produced a much nicer effect. Yet at the time, no one was using 12V to light. Thus there were no fixtures.

So I had to design my own.

Now, I was no artist. I was a mechanic and electrician. My fixtures were not fancy lanterns or blown-glass baubles. They were devices composed of simple straight lines, made of materials like tomato cans and mayonnaise jars. (I was "recycling" long before it became chic.) Because I was lighting up the gorgeous lawns and gardens of fancy houses, I would disguise or hide the fixtures, choosing instead to focus on the light and its effects.

This early necessity led me to my motto, which has served me and Nightscaping for more than forty years: *See the effect, not the source.*

This maxim was meant to apply strictly to lighting, but I think it covers other kinds of business, too. Generally, you'll want to concentrate on effects (the specific service and/or product you offer) rather than on the source (the means by which you get it done, or externals meant to make your business "look good"). People who spend too much time worrying about the image of their fledging business often lose sight of the most important part, which is providing something of value to customers/clients.

I certainly thought more about how to refine my outdoor lighting systems than I did about the image of my nascent company. In fact, I didn't even come up with the brand name! That was suggested by a friend of mine, Chris Barnes, who worked at the local newspaper. "Nightscaping," however, immediately seemed right. From that point on, it's been my trademark and is associated with all my patents. This, I would say, is also an example of resourcefulness—harnessing the brain power of a friend to come up with something for which today some people might look to a professional marketer.

United States Patent Office

770,661
Registered June 2, 1964

PRINCIPAL REGISTER
Trademark

Ser. No. 169,146, filed May 17, 1963

NIGHTSCAPING

William J. Locklin, doing business as Loran
5th Ave. and Walnut Road
Redlands, Calif.

For: ELECTRICAL FIXTURES AND PARTS EMPLOYED IN ILLUMINATING LANDSCAPED AREAS — NAMELY, ILLUMINATING FIXTURES, CABLES AND TRANSFORMERS—in CLASS 21.
First use July 10, 1962; in commerce Feb. 4, 1963.

Registering the Nightscaping trademark

The company's present location is also a function of finding something of value for a relatively low cost. In 1949 we'd moved the Quonset hut with us to Redlands, planting it in an run-down old orange grove. As my lighting business got off the ground, with me selling stock and fixtures, etc., the Quonset hut was no longer enough.

This time I found an abandoned packing house, renting it out for a very reasonable rate. Even though I'd already sold stock in the company, sales were only trickling in and cash was extremely tight. This is another thing young people should recognize—not only does entrepreneurship require resourcefulness, it requires persistence. And persistent resourcefulness. In some cases, it's not just one lean year, or two. It may be five, it may be ten. This is why it's a good idea to make sure you love what you're doing.

In any case, this packing house has served me for more than thirty years. I rented it for a while, then bought it outright in 1956. After that I slowly acquired more of the surrounding property and buildings. After 15 years I found myself in possession of five acres of industrial property and eight buildings. And this is where I work to this day.

As I grew the business in that old packing house, much of my task involved publicizing and explaining Nightscaping to the electrical industry. After all, these were my people, this was my field. I did sales and promotion everywhere I went: conferences, conventions, etc. It was hard work. Putting the product out through electrical distributors wasn't working. Electricians were very, very busy in the postwar boom and just weren't interested in new concepts as simple as 12V lighting. And the architects I talked to couldn't even understand what I was selling.

"What the hell is 12-volt?" was a common refrain.

This exhausting sales work coincided with a tough period for us. The first few years of Nightscaping were an extremely slow period for growth. I often had trouble meeting my payroll. However, I persisted. And, as is usually the case, by persisting I ended up receiving help from an unexpected place.

One day I got a call from a nursery in Cupertino—northern California—that had heard about my product and wanted to order fixtures directly from me. The man running this business, Itsu Uneka, offered to buy $300 worth of my product. With that I could just cover Friday's payroll, so I agreed.

Over the next few months, Itsu Uneka repeatedly helped me make payroll, which got me through one of the toughest times in my business career. I will always remember this man, and this bit of luck, that carried me through.

The experience also helped me realize I was marketing to the wrong group. At the time, electricians weren't really thinking of the need I was addressing. They didn't immediately grasp the significance of 12V's much-improved lighting effect. There was, however, a group that did care a great deal about the aesthetics of outdoor lighting: the green industry. This would be my new target market.

Sure enough, the outlet of gardeners and landscape architects really charged up my business. I had a great edge: no one then was providing the service or products I was. These days, people say to me, "Bill, must have been real nice not having any competition." Well, it wasn't all peaches and cream. Being a resourceful pioneer carried its own difficulties.

The "green" industry helped a great deal

I spent many years trying to find a market. Explaining myself and my product over and over. In return I received endless variations of "What the hell is 12-volt?", along with a few strange looks and more than one brush-off. So yes, I had no competition. I also had no market. I had to create one, convince these distributors to stock my unknown product. To have faith in an unknown idea. And what happened the moment I accomplished this, bringing 12-volt lighting into mainstream acceptance?

All of a sudden I had competitors. A lot of them. Many were knockoff artists based somewhere offshore. Cheap products, deficient, but nonetheless, competition.

Am I bitter about it? No way. My persistence paid off, even though it opened the gates to all these imitators.

So it goes.

Another test of my patience involved the long, long process of convincing electrical inspection authorities that my product was safe. Getting the approval of such entities as the city of Los Angeles, the Underwriters Laboratories, and the Canadian Standards Association took many years. When approval did come, however, our dogged efforts often proved to be worth it. The UL, for instance, adopted our work, our own protocols, as its standard for the entire low-voltage landscape lighting industry (#1838).

Not a bad selling point.

Once business picked up, shipping became an issue. Not an easy one to solve. In the fifties, when we started out, advanced, foolproof global shipping systems (such as those of today's UPS or FedEx) did not exist. In those days many small business such as ourselves relied upon Greyhound buses.

These buses would deliver packages for you, and since they went across the country, station by station, you could get them to almost any town you needed. Coast to coast, the service took five to seven days, which isn't all that bad compared to something like the current ground service from UPS.

Yet there were serious drawbacks to Greyhound package delivery. In one case, we'd sold a good deal of lights to a customer who needed them in place immediately, for a wedding reception. Well, we packed the delivery onto the good old Greyhound and, wouldn't you know it, the thing got in a bad accident and caught fire. Of course in such a case the lights in the cargo compartment aren't what you're most concerned with, but it did represent a serious challenge to our business. So we began searching for other means of delivery, steadily improving the methods by which we shipped our product to our customers. Which eventually provided me with one of the biggest, and simplest, thrills of my entire working life.

One day, driving down a random street in Los Angeles, I happened to glimpse a delivery truck with the back end open. And there, in the back of the truck, was a carton with *Nightscaping* printed on the side. Let me tell you, I felt then as if I'd arrived—as if all the scraping and hustling I'd done, all the never-say-die pushes, had finally paid off. Of course, there was still plenty of hard work ahead.

As any good businessperson knows, resourcefulness and persistence aren't qualities needed only at the beginning of a career—they must be sustained throughout. They're as important to an 85-year-old as they were to the enterprising 30-year-old he once was. Trust me on that.

Concepts

- **Resourcefulness** should be the linchpin of most strategies employed by fledgling businesses.

- **Creativity is a basic requirement** for anyone who'd like to build a business from the ground up. If you're not someone who likes to invent, figure out new ways to do things, or improvise around traditional themes, you might want to rethink your future ambitions.

- **Getting some space of your own**, a stage for your ideas, is a key element of small-business success. The practical advantages of this step are matched by a set of psychological advantages—i.e., a "workshop" or office of any type lends credibility and legitimacy to the undertaking, both in the eyes of others and in your own mind.

- **Focus on developing and exploiting your strengths**, rather than on acquiring all the trappings of a successful business. One major aspect of resourcefulness is learning what's important and what's not important. Only the crucial elements of your business should receive the attention of your hard-won and limited capital.

- **Stripped-down is a good way to proceed**. No, I'm not talking about your birthday suit. Even big businesses are moving toward a greater focus on "core competencies." As an emerging business, you'll need to narrow this focus to a laser-like intensity, isolating exactly what you do better, what your edge is, then exploiting it over and over.

- **Persistence** is not an option—it's a necessity. If you're someone who gets discouraged easily, or if you quickly tire of repetitive activities, you'll want to think twice about starting your own business. It may seem exciting, even glamorous, to work for yourself, setting your own hours, etc. Much of running your own business can be drudgework, however—whether we're talking about filling out endless forms or mopping the shop floor.

- You're also going to **butt your head against strong forces**. The market is a tough place; there are no honest get-rich-quick methods. Even if your product or service is of the highest class, even if it's revolutionary, you're going up against one of two basic forces: one, competition, if you're selling something established; or two, the unknown, if you're selling something new. The latter is generally the higher of the two obstacles. Only with persistence can you surmount them.

10 Reflection Questions

1. What kind of space do you need to begin your business? If you had ten million dollars in start-up funds, what kind of space would you acquire? What aspects of this ideal can be applied to the space available with your real budget?

2. What are the essential elements of your business? What is it that you do that no one else does?

3. What resources do you need to run and grow your business? Which ones are available through non-traditional channels?

4. Are there any free or low-cost resources (think media, manpower, materials) you're neglecting?

5. Are you spending time and money on any non-essential business activities? (I.e., is the logo design really worth a new computer program and three days of your time?)

6. Are you willing to work sixty hours a week for a minimum of five years without any profit to show for it? This may be necessary just to keep your business afloat.

7. Are you a tenacious person, who won't take no for an answer, or do you tend to accept negative responses? The world, for a new business owner, most often seems like a universal "NO!"; you must be able to resist this.

8. Do you believe in your product/service enough to be evangelical about it? Or are you just thinking this is something that will make you a buck? The latter attitude will tire and give up much, much earlier than the first, and for good reason.

9. How well do you handle real adversity? In other words, how quickly do you bounce back? For a small business owner, the "deflate" time has to be nearly nil, as you'll need to address crises on your feet, quickly. The universe will hand you some pretty rough deals from time to time.

10. Realistically speaking, how innovative are you? How creative? New businesses are about taking the initiative. There are no maps to follow, so you need to be the type of person who likes to explore. Bravely.

Chapter 3

Follow Your Instincts . . . . and Interests

My Story

To understand how I got where I am today, it's important for you to know that I took several "detours." By this I mean that at certain points in my life I turned off the main track. In each instance this turn greatly influenced my life and my future career. And in each instance I made the turn as a result of my instincts, my interests, or both.

It is these turns that help us become what, and who, we want to be. On the other hand, some turns lead only into dead ends, and lead us away from where, what, and who we want to be. I'm not saying I always turned the right way. But I do know that some of the bigger choices I made in my life led to me sitting here, in this chair, rather than to a job I didn't like, or a jail cell, or even an early grave.

The first big choice I made was to leave high school before graduation.

This might surprise you, but I really had no problem with school. I know, the usual story of a dropout who becomes successful is different: "I had no time for school/was bored/didn't fit in." And so on. While these things might have been true part of the time, they certainly weren't overriding factors for me. So let me explain what did actually precipitate me leaving school, and why I think it was a wise choice.

See, it wasn't the work; I actually liked most of the subjects. And, if an eleventh-grade dropout may be allowed to brag for a moment, I would say I excelled in them. In the schoolwork part, that is. Though I had calmed down by this point in my life, I still had a mouth on me.

One teacher in particular wouldn't take my sass. In one class, tired of the comments I chose to share with my peers, this lady smacked me right on the ear. Then, as I was falling out of my seat, she grabbed me by that same ear and jerked me upright. After about the third time this happened I got the point. Believe me, I never sassed that lady again. Especially after she became my mother-in-law.

Her daughter, a year older than me, was currently enrolled at a local community college. We fell in love, and in the heat of things decided to run off to Yuma, Arizona to get married. Which we did.

The year was 1939. Things were starting to look a little bleak in Europe, to say the least. I was now a married man and fully expected to soon be a father. After our excursion I was out of money and had no job. With these types of responsibility, staying in school no longer seemed like a viable option.

So I took a job at the Palm Springs racquet club. I worked as a lifeguard, though I couldn't even swim. I was, however, a good-looking, husky young lad. The notables appreciated this, sometimes commenting on it as I brought them their drinks and towels. I suppose this is why I made some pretty good money at the old racquet club.

So this work was fine for a while, but once my first daughter arrived, in 1940, it was time to find a real, honest job. Being a craggy old man handing out towels and martinis somehow didn't appeal to me.

After a bit of looking around I managed to pull down a job as an electrician's helper at the Colton Portland Cement Company, which was already 50 years old at the time, and which is now remembered as the founding location of the California Portland Cement Company, a huge operation that spans much of the US west.

I worked on the plant's enormous industrial controls for a while, learning quite a bit over the few months I was there, but then something bigger came along.

World War II.

I enlisted in the Navy early, serving for the entire US portion of the war, nearly five years, on submarines in the Pacific. I entered the Navy as an electrician's mate, third class, and came out chief electrician's mate. Not a bad spot of training.

A close-up of my mug during WWII

In addition to getting my first glimpse of the Quonset huts, one of which would become my future office, I also acquired a taste for adventure during the war years. Suddenly, returning to Colton Cement to work the graveyard shift no longer sounded very appetizing.

So I decided, for the second time in my life (the first was leaving high school to get married), to turn off the beaten path and start off on my own. *But what should I do?* As I was trying to figure it out, I took the California electrical contractor's license exam and began wiring the tract houses. And thus my career began, while I wasn't really looking.

The tract wiring jobs and my little retail business in the Quonset hut kept me busy for the next five years or so, until my instincts and interests kicked up again and wouldn't let me rest until I heeded them. I came up with an idea and began trying to convince my wife and my daughters, eleven and five at the time, into selling our home, renting out the Quonset hut, buying a 30-foot trailer, and touring the United States.

Somehow I got them to agree. So we set off, at the beginning of the 1950s, into America. We drove from town to town, from union hall to union hall. In many of them I would find work. And in each town we would all learn something new about America, about life, and about ourselves. It was on this trip that I met the traffic-jam fisherman, for instance.

For three years we stayed on the road. After that it was time to return to California. We all had much wider perspectives, and I was armed with a great deal of knowledge I'd acquired by working on a wide variety of jobs.

When we returned, settling in the friendly community of Redlands, California, I moved the Quonset hut from Colton and got right back into business. At this point I specialized in industrial motor controls: wind machines, deep-well pumps, frost control for packing houses, etc. I wasn't much interested in doing the tract houses or any individual house calls at all—"housework," as I called it, didn't really excite me.

After a while I realized, however, that some of the successful homeowners around me had houses that resembled industrial buildings, in terms of complexity, more than they resembled the tract houses with which I'd grown so bored. Being the breadwinner of my family, I also wasn't blind to the fact that installing a new dining room fixture or cutting a plug for something called a "television" (a strange device with a ten-inch screen, which all the neighbors were flocking in to see) for these homeowners could be good for my career and for our immediate financial state.

One of the common requests homeowners would come up with was that I install some type of outdoor lighting. In those days the range of options were limited. All outdoor/landscaping lighting was done with 120-volt currents. The means for doing this were often provided by reflector lamps being developed to light outdoor billboards, such as the PAR-38 from GE. These waterproof lamps required no fixtures and soon became the accepted standard for outdoor lighting.

Yet I was dissatisfied with the effect produced. The light seemed extremely harsh and didn't sit well with the aesthetic sense I'd developed while handling the outdoor stage lighting at the Redlands Bowl. There I used scrims and gels, producing the effects I wanted from lights that were not meant to be seen.

Hmmm.

Slowly an idea took root. What about lighting people's properties the same way? With fixtures and light sources that weren't the center of the picture, I could manipulate the effects to a greater extent. *After all, it's the light we're after. That's what really makes the landscapes beautiful.*

I began experimenting with a number of different fixtures, using whatever materials I had on hand or whatever I could scavenge. I didn't worry about how they looked, concentrating instead on the quality of light produced. I used a car battery as a power source and found the harsh effects of 120-volt light largely mitigated by the 12-volt current. I tweaked my improvised fixtures, creations of tomato cans and mayonnaise jars, until I could make the light do exactly what I wanted.

After a while I hit upon the principle that's served as my company motto to this very day: *See the effect, not the source.*

This isn't all to say that my interests and instincts have always and unfailingly led me in profitable or even productive directions. They haven't and shouldn't be expected to. The trick, however, is to not lose faith in them.

For instance, I once became interested in doing some hydroponic growing of vegetables. This seemed as if it could be very profitable, and the run-down orange trees in my run-down grove weren't producing anything in any case.

So I cleared out a section of the grove, removing the orange trees and leveling the ground. In this area I constructed greenhouses measuring twenty by a hundred feet. After that I went to all the state-school courses on hydroponic growing that I could find.

After my study I began with tomatoes and cucumbers, which shot up and grew ripe and plump. *Gorgeous.* Once the crop was in, it was time to figure out what to do with it. At first I took my vegetables to Los Angeles, where there was a wholesale produce district. Then another thought occurred.

Why not just sell retail from my "ranch"?

So I did. In the grove I put together a selling area called the "Tomato Patch." It was an immediate success. So I decided to grow it, putting in a small petting zoo and a BBQ area. On Saturday and Sunday I served breakfasts—eggs, pancakes, you name it. Things were going swimmingly. On my way to Knott's Berry farm, I was.

Then my good friends in the county board of supervisors decided to get involved. Couldn't have an upstart business taking off like this without dipping their hands in. They came to the conclusion that because I was in an agricultural preserve, I could legally sell only what I raised. Much bickering and legal expense followed.

In the end the board of supervisors won. I had to close the tomato patch, and it never rose again. I do, however, still run across the occasional man or woman who tells me they remember coming to the tomato patch as kids. "Boy, it was fun!" is the universal refrain. Which makes the whole thing a sweeter memory than it would otherwise be.

So while not all the moves I've made in my life, the sharp turns off the beaten path, have borne fruit, many of them have. And all of them, from marrying my wife in 1939 to refusing to return to the cement factory and buying a Quonset hut in 1946 to taking over a stage lighting job upon my settling in Redlands—all of them have made me who I am today.

In 1974 my beautiful, faithful wife of 35 years was taken from me after a struggle with incurable cancer. Twenty-one years later my oldest daughter passed away. These were the two companions of my earliest adult years, who I came to know and love through the grace of my best instincts. The wonderful life I began with them was waiting for me just one step off the beaten path, and I shall be forever grateful to have taken it.

Concepts

- **Following your instincts** is an essential ingredient of business success, as we're often smarter than we give ourselves credit for. If something feels wrong, in other words, it probably is.

- **What you're interested in** should be a key determinant of what you do with yourself.

- Becoming an independent entrepreneur is hard work, sometimes backbreaking, and the **long hours and extreme dedication required can stretch on for years**. Thus, if you're not truly interested in what you're doing, your chances of holding on through the hard times will be severely diminished.

- **Doing "the same as everyone else does"** is more of a pattern for business failure than success.

- While some elements of successful businesses practices may, and should, be copied, it's your **differences** that you want to focus on and isolate.

- Otherwise known as your advantage or "edge," **it's the differences**—the offshoots of your individual interests and instincts—**that set you apart from the competition**.

- Not all of the choices you make will end in success, but the most important thing is to **keep believing in your own instinct and interests**. In the end, the sum of these choices will be the person you become—the more you have the courage to make, the stronger you'll be when all is said and done.

10 Reflection Questions

1. When you were a child, besides the obvious, what kinds of things captivated you?

2. What activities, subjects, or ideas truly excite you now?

3. If you could dedicate yourself to any task you wished for the next twenty years, what would it be?

4. How often do you make spontaneous decisions based upon feelings?

5. How effective are you at untangling the "common" or "usual" or "obvious" thing to do from what feels right to you? In other words, how susceptible are you to what's known as "group think"?

6. Do you agree with the following statement: though necessary to run a successful business, common sense can, paradoxically, occasionally be the wrong guide to follow?

7. How comfortable are you with expressing your differences among others, or taking a stance that conflicts with a majority opinion?

8. How much confidence in your own decisions do you have? Do you tend to adjust to other people's points of view rather than fully explicating yours? If the answers to the above are "not much" and "yes," how can you begin presenting your own case in a clearer and more assertive fashion?

9. At what points in your life have you diverged from a common path by conscious choice? What was the result in each of these cases?

10. Think of the assertive people you know, those who seem to follow their own instincts and interests a bit more than the average person. What positive statements can you make about their mindsets? What can you learn from them?

Chapter 4

Search for Knowledge

My Story

Nothing I know of approaches the value of knowledge when it comes to beginning and maintaining a successful business. Simply put, those who know more, do more. Those who know less, do less.

When your operation's first getting off the ground, there is no such thing as specialization. You're forced to do nearly everything yourself. And to do it properly, you must first learn it. There's nothing worse than a bunch of signs of mediocrity hung around your fledgling enterprise—trust me, they will drive people away.

So you have to be good at everything.

This requirement doesn't stop once you're off the ground, either. Sure, maybe you'll be wildly successful and able to take on the role of absentee boss, hiring someone to oversee the business on a day-to-day basis. Still, you'll want to know as much as you can about the different aspects of your business—or else the first indication of something going wrong might be a big dip in the bottom line.

Besides, it's so much more fun to keep your hands in the machinery! There's a very practical advantage to being able to fill, or at least assist with, many of the roles in your business—from shipping to marketing to computers, and so on. In the early years, it will often be a day-to-day struggle for survival we're talking about. Unfortunately, perfect attendance or occupational fidelity is not something you can count on as an employer.

Checking plans from the design department

I've always been a seeker of knowledge. Even though I dropped out of high school, I found many of the subjects compelling. After the war, while I traveled the United States with my family, stopping at union halls for electrician work, we did all we could to soak up the knowledge connected to the areas in which we found ourselves.

In Springfield, Illinois we became experts on Abraham Lincoln, as I worked on a 30-day contract. In the desert around Los Alamos, New Mexico, we spent a great deal of time together learning about the local Native Americans and their culture.

As for my profession: my formal electric training began, I suppose, with the industrial controls of the cement plant in Colton. Here I learned about the high-voltage side of the game, I learned about motor control, and I learned safety. Then, of course, I spent nearly five years as an electrical technician on a little underwater boat, where an electrical failure could obviously cost us a lot more than a night of television.

This was an education in itself.

Some hardware I found in the Pacific

When I returned from the Pacific, I broadened my skills still more by doing the tract house wiring—which really wasn't that difficult. Soon I returned to industrial motor controls, doing contract work for some very fine local commercial vineyards and agricultural operations. After my three-year America tour I started moving away from the tract jobs, developing my specialties—motor controls, wind machines, deep-well pumps, and frost control—in earnest. Before too long I had three employees working for me. And perhaps then I began to think, erroneously of course, that I could handle any kind of electrical project thrown at me.

Overconfidence is a common pitfall for any kind of skilled worker or independent businessperson, especially those who work in fields where the available knowledge is nearly unlimited. I would say the most dangerous period, as regards overconfidence or "biting off more than you can chew," comes at the point where you've learned a fair amount, have put in maybe three to five years of good work handling tough projects in which you dealt successfully with difficult obstacles, but still haven't quite learned enough to be scared of how much you don't know.

In the late 1940s the US government was testing its aeronautics equipment on the ground. They did this through the use of "rocket sleds"—small rocket-propelled cars that ran on rail-like tracks thousands of feet long. Much of this early work was going on at Edwards Air Force base, in the Mojave desert at the edge of Los Angeles county. The government was accepting bids for the project.

Very confident of my electrical abilities, I bid on one aspect of the project: the telemetering, which had to do with taking measurements (of the vehicle, passenger, or just about anything) remotely. I must have convinced someone I could do it, because my bid was eventually selected.

After a three-hour drive to the job site from my house, it didn't take me long to figure out that I was in over my head. Way over my head. I didn't have the requisite skills or knowledge to do what I needed to do, plain and simple, and I sure as hell wasn't going to be able to acquire them during the seven-week job period.

In the end, I had to find and hire a cable splicer to bail me out. This was a very costly arrangement. Every day for seven solid weeks, I made a three-hour drive into the desert, worked for 10 hours, and then drove three hours home. In addition to being exhausting, this period ended up losing me more than $500 total—a sum I could ill afford at the time. Nevertheless, it could have been worse.

I learned an important lesson in this fiasco. Which was that not every job would be self-evident—some would require knowledge and skill that I couldn't just "learn on the fly." This may seem like a simple lesson, but in fact before that I'd just taken it as a matter-of-fact truth that I'd have to learn on each job. Not until the government project in the desert did I learn the true dangers of not looking before leaping. Taking jobs for which you're unprepared or "skill-deficient" can sink your business. Quickly.

Knowledge and skills in business are one thing; a wide perspective on the world itself is another. One tangential lesson I draw from my own early experience is that it's absolutely imperative for young people get out and experience all that they can. Learning some of the depth of the world in general can actually help shield a young entrepreneur from some of the mistakes associated with naiveté.

It wasn't long after the rocket sled episode that I packed the family up and began the cross-country trip that would last three years. Much of the purpose behind this expedition was to gain new knowledge—both of the country and of my profession. And that's exactly what happened.

In one of our early stops—Denver—I worked on the original Stapleton Airfield. The man I worked with was, quite literally, an artist when it came to bending large wire conduit. From him I learned to calculate radius so that these pipes would nest together in a very efficient and aesthetically pleasing arrangement. This may sound simple, but such techniques were not common at the time, and they not only made for very beautiful installations, but also led to easy wire pulling when the time came.

From Denver we found our way to Los Alamos, New Mexico. There I worked on Building D, which was part of the Manhattan Project. It was the original plutonium processing facility, which, because of its radioactivity, was dubbed by some of its researchers "the hottest place in town." Needless to say, I learned quite a bit more about intricate control systems there in the desert, where the atomic age officially began.

Eventually we drove our trailer east, and this is how we found ourselves on the road to Birmingham, where we encountered the traffic trout-fisherman. Once we arrived in town, I was immediately hired as an electrician foreman for a local company. Great job, and I was pleased as punch for all of the two weeks that it lasted.

I'd been filling the position quite effectively, but that didn't matter. The owner of the company, upon learning I was a high-school dropout, said he couldn't have someone without even a *college* education in such an important role. I didn't agree, but no matter—I was out of a job again, and in possession of a new, painful indicator of the value of education.

It wasn't until I started my own company, and until that company began turning a regular profit, that I truly escaped the monkey on my back that was my early decision to leave high school. People can say what they want about "it's who you know that counts," but I truly believe it's what you know that counts. And all the situations I've seen that turn on a high school or college diploma have only strengthened this belief.

As a business owner I've taken pains to learn about every aspect of my operation, even down to the manufacturing process. Over the past few decades I've taken it upon myself to learn about sand-casting aluminum, which involves pouring molten aluminum into patterns pressed into a fine sand mixture.

Brass pouring

I've learned about casting red brass and yellow brass; I've learned about the hand-spinning methods of stainless steel and copper production; I've learned about CNC lathes and presses that spin the metals through the guidance of a computer.

A spinning machine

I've learned all about powder coating (and the disasters it can cause). I even learned the basics of computers, which for a man born in 1921 is fairly unusual, I think. These technical challenges have been variously exciting, funny, and painful, but, looking back, this old technician has to say they've been pretty enjoyable overall.

One of my most interesting skill acquisitions has been that of night photography in subdued lighting conditions. Once Nightscape got off the ground, I naturally wanted to record some of the beautiful installations we'd done in California for promotional purposes. So I "perfected" the technical side of the process, then let the camera and the lighting do the rest, simply making sure I got everything I wanted in the frame.

However, it wasn't only the technical aspect of photography I needed to learn about. It wasn't simply a lack of shutter knowledge that led me into some interesting—but also embarrassing, disappointing, and ultimately costly—mistakes.

For instance. One of my contractor customers (the Nightscaping products are sold to independent distributors and landscapers) once informed me of a beautiful job he'd done up in the Hollywood Hills. We decided that I'd come and photograph the results, thinking the publicity would be good for the both of us.

When I arrived at the appointed place and time, I found a gorgeous house, and quickly began setting up my tripod for some long-exposure shots. The scene was, indeed, beautiful. So beautiful it took me a few minutes to notice the gorgeous tropical swimming pool a bit behind my position. Once I saw it, however, it didn't take me long to notice the half-dozen or so night swimmers enjoying themselves in it. Naked.

Concentrating on the job at hand, after that, was difficult. Especially since the unclothed folks in the pool had also noticed my presence, and were calling out, tauntingly, for me to come join them. *Keep your eye on the picture, Bill.*

A more serious photographic issue down the road stemmed from a fundamental ignorance on my part. I'd taken some night shots of a gorgeous set-up up done by another contractor, and used them for commercial (advertising) purposes. Problem was, I hadn't thought to request a property release from the owner of the house. Thus I didn't have permission to use photos of his house. So I was sued and eventually had to fork over what added up to a weekend trip to the Bahamas for a family of four.

Never did that again.

In addition to these two notable experiences, I remember countless instances in which I felt my fingers were going to freeze off (hard to manipulate the switches with gloves on), or returning with a roll of film only to find out the exposure timing or aperture had been set wrong. Many times I came home after a long night with nothing. Oh, how I regret that I had to do all this in the days before digital cameras made it a snap.

Yet these were all bumps in the learning process of a skill which has enhanced my business immeasurably. Did I have the money to hire a professional photographer in those days? No. Were pictures of the glorious lighting effects that could be obtained through my products crucial to my business success? Yes.

So I had to do it myself. And this is the way, in my opinion, that the world at large is going. Young people just starting out need to have a wide range of skills to be able to compete, let alone start a business. With all the technology available to average people these days—computers being the most obvious example—there's a much wider range of tasks that can be achieved by an entrepreneur willing to learn, many of them in the realm of advertising and marketing (here I'm thinking of websites and desktop publishing), but most in the core business itself.

It's an "on-demand" world, as they say. Today, when a 40-foot semi and trailer loaded with five-inch diameter ABS pipe pulls into our complex, I'm reminded of what I had to do in the early days. We use this pipe, made of thermoplastic resin that weathers burial in the soil exceptionally well, for ground fittings, cutting it here in the factory into eight-inch sections.

When we first started out, however, things were different. In those days I had to drive to Los Angeles to pick up a 20-foot section of this pipe, which they would cut in half for me. Then I'd bring it back here, and we'd cut it into the eight-inch sections. Not to say this didn't work well. Allowing for the saw marks, we'd end up using every single millimeter of that pipe, wasting nothing.

Part of the search for knowledge, in a business sense, has to do with a willingness to be an "early adopter"—that is, to try new technologies that may provide you with an edge over the competition. Yet this, too, has its pitfalls.

Once we'd acquired mainstream credibility, and, with it, dozens of "knock-off" competitors, I tried to use whatever technological innovations I thought would help us get a leg up in the market we'd created. That's part of being a pioneering business, the way I see it. If you're always in the lead, you force other companies to adapt to you, rather than vice-versa. This is a strong position to be in.

Yet it can also make for a harrowing ride.

In 1967 there came, out of Australia, a new innovation in industrial painting applications. This new technique, known as "powder coating," ended the process by which paint was applied as a solid suspended in liquids (which must evaporate for the paint to "dry"). There were several technical advantages to the former process, which I won't go into here, and as a result we were the first in our industry to adopt powder coating.

Just as we'd set up our powder-coat line of products in 1986, the Challenger space shuttle exploded over Cape Canaveral in Florida. As it turns out, the company we'd contracted to supply our powder coating had also supplied NASA with some of the parts for Challenger. There was some concern that one of the parts this company made contributed to the accident. Talk about bad publicity!

Of course, with worries like these, this company (which will remain nameless here) didn't care too much about any problems we might have with our new line of powder coat products. We were at the bottom of their list.

The first sign of a problem with the new line came in the form of a call from our Florida distributor (another Challenger coincidence), who complained to me that he'd just opened a carton of plastic-sealed fixtures and found them all rusted.

I assured him it must be some kind of mistake and told him to go ahead and open another carton. Sure enough, he found six rusted fixtures still in their original shrink wrap. This is how I first learned of the failure of our powder-coat line.

Before I could get the situation under control, we'd produced three-month's worth of faulty fixtures. All of them either rusted in the box or did so shortly after being placed out in the weather. Needless to say, our competition had a field day with this. I don't even want to relate how much this episode cost the company; let me just say we replaced every bad fixture for no charge, sent new ones in response to every complaint, and paid for the freight ourselves. We recovered, but such are the perils of searching for knowledge and becoming an "early adopter" or industry leader.

A more successful example involves our "IQ control system," which I developed in close consultation with contractors and their clients. To produce an effective control system, in addition to understanding how to light houses, I also had to understand *why* people wanted their houses lit. This would help me figure out the best, most user-friendly control system. (The question of "Why Light?" has been a guiding influence behind my business practices, and one we'll discuss more fully in a later chapter.)

Our initial IQ control system worked decently for a while—it was better than nothing and kept us ahead of the competition. Still, it was a first-generation device and very flawed. Our contractors found so many faults in this system that we had to discontinue it.

As a replacement we eventually came up with "The Dominator," a low-voltage control with four remote low-voltage motion sensors as well as a photocell and timer. This system has been exceptionally well-received as a security item, a convenience, and as an aesthetic enhancement. However, as is so often the case, we've already seen signs of an offshore knock-off. Such is the condition of those who learn, and search for knowledge, in order to innovate.

I've become thick-skinned about it, though. Better to smile than to snarl. So I've accepted the idea that copying is the highest form of flattery—and also a strong sign of success.

Concepts

- As a budding entrepreneur, you'll find that **knowledge will be your most important asset**. It may sound clichéd, but it's always true.

- Without an expansion of your knowledge base, your business will founder. **A good idea to start with isn't enough.** You must consistently learn, both to keep ahead of any competition and to satisfy the market you're trying to serve.

- **Developing a wide range of divergent skills,** becoming proficient at tasks such as desktop publishing or web design, will allow you to sharply reduce start-up costs and overhead. Wasting money up front is one of the easiest ways to sink a new business.

- A successful owner will generally **keep her hands in the machinery** of her enterprise. Especially at the beginning. Learning all the various aspects of your business allows you to quickly identify trouble spots and occasionally to fill in for those performing critical roles.

- It's very important, at the same time, **to know your limitations,** the boundaries of your knowledge and abilities. Taking on too much can lead to disasters and occasionally start wicked chain reactions. Believing you can "do anything" is the opposite of knowledge.

- **Don't stick to too narrow a field of study.** You may think you simply need to know about one area, such as computers or manufacturing, to succeed. In fact, the more depth with which you see the world, the better off you'll be in business. Naiveté can devastate a business.

- **Continued innovation is the hallmark of a durable business.** I've lasted for more than 40 years. And I'm still out looking for new technical advances, new ways to improve our product.

- **Being an innovator, or industry leader, also carries risks.** There are reasons people act conservatively in the business world; there's nothing new under the sun, and most unorthodox start-up ideas are simply eccentric takes on flawed business plans. Change brings risk, and the "ain't broke-don't fix" admonition rings true in many ears. Thus a balance must be struck between a positive, deliberate creative path and wild instability.

- **Don't be overly worried about imitation or competition.** If your ideas are good enough to copy, you'll do fine. Take it as flattery and affirmation.

10 Reflection Questions

1. What do you find yourself most eager to learn about? What bores you to tears? If the answer to the second question involves a critical aspect of a potential business, think twice about your plans.

2. What kind of owner do you see yourself being? A hands-on, detail-oriented type (think George Steinbrenner) or an absentee boss who delegates, shoots off brilliant ideas, and then escapes for two-hour lunches and a game of tennis? (It's a trick question. The second type doesn't exist. At least not in the world of start-up entrepreneurship.)

3. Are you willing to do the "lowest" job duty of your lowest-level employee? If not, maybe you'd be better off in a corporate suite.

4. Are you inspired when encountering new information, or does it leave you cold?

5. How easily can you translate recently gained knowledge into action and real-world results?

6. Do you feel comfortable learning new skills and doing good, even professional-level work in a divergent range of fields? Or are you comfortable only in one narrow range of skill sets?

7. Assuming you have one or more ideas right now for a prospective business, which one can you see most obviously developing into a "forty-year challenge"? I.e., what will fascinate you, allow for the most innovation, and deserve the attention of your abilities and working life for the long-haul?

8. What's your general level of intellectual curiosity with regards to the larger world? (For most ultra-successful entrepreneurs, the answer is "extremely high.")

9. Are you comfortable with the risks inherent in the adoption of new ideas? Can you handle a setback based on a new idea without becoming overly conservative?

10. The other side of the coin, with regards to too narrow a focus, is the tendency to dabble. Can you stay focused *enough* on one thing to carry through with your plans? Or are you attracted (and distracted) by too many fields and interests?

Chapter 5

Success Is *Mañana*

My Story

First, before I get into what the above motto's meant to me over the years, I suppose I should explain what it means in literal terms. The word *mañana* means *morning* or *tomorrow* in Spanish. Thus the half-English, half-Spanish phrase above would be literally translated as "Success is Tomorrow."

A start, but not quite coherent.

I suppose the easiest, and most recognizable, form of this idea would be that in business—and remember, I'm speaking here mainly to people who are starting their own—you're always thinking about the future. But there's more to it than that.

For many the ideas of *mañana* conjures up a shrug of the shoulders and someone telling you that while the work may or may not be done tomorrow, it certainly won't be done today. There is another sense, however, and this is the one I think of when this phrase winds its way through my head.

The word *mañana* can also mean "look to tomorrow" or "the future with optimism." This is the way I see it. Not that work will be put off until tomorrow, but that by considering the future well, planning for it, and not asking for everything today, we'll encounter our success *mañana*.

Not to sound like a stodgy old-timer, but from my point of view it seems a lot of young people today have gotten it into their heads that success is something that comes suddenly, overnight, and that riches and all other kinds of fulfillment that signify it come in the blink of an eye, once you've gotten that perfect idea and taken a few baby steps toward making it into reality. A few are a bit more realistic, and go further than this—actually creating something.

Still, all too often these folks rent a building, put up a sign, take an ad out in the yellow pages, and expect success to come tumbling down on them. Sorry, but that ain't how it works. Faced with a deafening silence, the one that almost always follows the opening of a new, untested business, many of these slightly unrealistic entrepreneurs simply give up, or lose the will to fight through the beginning.

However, by always looking to tomorrow, or *mañana*, many of these issues can be avoided. Of course we live in the present, not the future, and your creditors generally won't accept checks dated two years in advance. However, though it may seem like a paradox, very often looking toward the future will keep your business exactly where it needs to be on a day-to-day level.

As you go about setting up your enterprise, you should be devoting a set amount of your time each day to addressing future needs and possibilities. This means you should be planning for long-range possibilities, preparing your business both for possible near—and mid-term successes and failures, making contingency plans, and brainstorming on enhancements you can make now that will help your business's growth, when it comes, be more robust and proceed more smoothly.

In short, you need to be envisioning the future. This is the toughest element of entrepreneurship for many people to grasp. They think, "Okay, I have this great service/product. People will love it. All I have to do is perfect it and sell it. The rest will fall into place." Unfortunately this isn't true.

Yes, we all know the myths of the "runaway business." The gold mine started by some single-minded mad genius in his basement or by some college kid in his dorm room. Ideas so good a massive and lucrative business formed itself around them. Do these examples exist in real life? Sure. Well, sort of.

I imagine if you questioned Bill Gates or Ted Turner or Mark Cuban about their early path to success, you'd find the road was a lot bumpier than their official capsule biographies let on. All of these men are known for their innovations, yet each one is also known for being a shrewd, even savage businessman, as well as being something of a visionary. "Seeing the future" always gives you a leg up on the competition and the marketplace.

On the other hand, failure to see the future will result in a fall, no matter how good your product. Thus the ancient saying can be amended: "Where the leaders (you) have no vision, the people (your enterprise and its employees) perish."

From beginning to end the idea is to work for tomorrow, to think for tomorrow, and to be patient with the thing called success. If you succeed in seeing what's going to happen *mañana*, than you'll find success *mañana*.

As for me, my current business began when I incorporated it in the state of California, long before I had any pressing reason to do so. Long before it was really much of a business. So when it came time to sell stock (a blunder we'll get to later—suffice to say, it took me 20 years to buy back all the stock once I sold it, though it's now all mine), when it came time for the business to grow and function as a larger entity, I was ready. The structure was already set up.

In the 1950s, as I worked as an electrical contractor and raised my family with my wife, my outdoor lighting manufacturing and installation was a hobby. After wiring a few dozen tract houses, I quickly realized there were more interesting things to do. I also realized the more interesting things paid better—specialty contractors were in higher demand than plain-old house wirers. So I began my focus on industrial systems—things like frost control, wind machines, deep-well pumps, and packing house equipment.

Soon I developed a reputation as a good industrial contractor. Did I have my eye on bigger things? Did I want to go further? Sure. I had my eye on *mañana*.

At the same time I knew that to be successful in the future, I needed to do my work *today* exceptionally well. This is another lesson that for me is wrapped up in the phrase "Success is Mañana." Do your job today, and do it right. Better than that, make sure all the expectations of your clients and customers are met and—as often as possible—exceeded. Do that, and you'll be almost assured of future success.

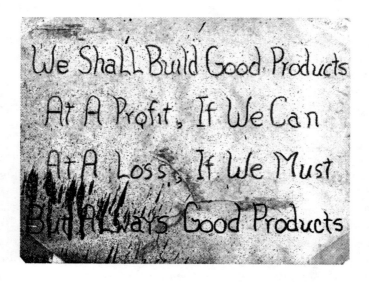

Early mission statement

It may seem like two contradictory ideas here—keeping your mind on the future and doing the best job you absolutely can *right now*. However, they're not exclusive. It's the poor strategy of doing "just enough" (to avoid litigation, sometimes), that hinders fledgling businesses. They don't understand that to survive, to draw new customers in a tough marketplace, they need to wow people. Or they can't see that to survive a down time they need to build up a sterling, remarkable reputation.

In short, they can't see the future, and this affects their work in the moment.

As I began fixing industrial problems encountered in Southern California, I slowly began realizing how successful the owners of these enterprises were. Called from time to time to do house calls (a lot of them had industrial-scale jobs in their homes, believe me), I soon saw the potential of these gorgeous pieces of property.

Ready to begin moving my contracting business upward and in the direction of my interests, not satisfied even with the considerable challenges and decent living of an industrial contractor, I started promoting my outdoor lighting skills to this select group. Some of them, as a result, hired me to light the beautiful grounds surrounding their beautiful houses. Though true success was still a long way away, I was confident and deeply engaged in the moment. I was thinking about *mañana*, yet concentrating on the work of the day.

In this period the ideas that would lead to Nightscaping were born.

A year or so later one of my clients in the Imperial Valley called. Actually, his ranch foreman did. The boss had a job for me, he said. A very special one that needed to be completed within two weeks.

Being that this was a good client, who always paid the bills on time and never quarreled about the price, I jumped at the chance. The project was for a massive outdoor lighting setup. After driving over and seeing the state of the estate, seeing the massive amount of work that needed to be done, I went straight to LA.

And immediately ran into problems. I talked to the distributor of the 120-V fixtures I needed for the lighting job. I talked to the manufacturer. Neither gave me any hope of getting the necessary lamps in time to do the job. This was a stopper.

So I headed straight for my workshop. This was an important client, and as any independent businessperson knows, it's these kinds of projects that make (or break) you. Simply turning around and saying, *Sorry, I can't do it*, wasn't an option.

In a flash I returned to my workshop and began experimenting. I'd already been messing around with low-voltage lighting configurations. My materials were simple: car headlamps and batteries, mayonnaise jars for lenses, painted coffee and tomato juice cans. Sometime in the middle of all my tinkering, I learned what this special lighting project was for: a big party. At about the same time I learned for whom the party was being thrown: President Dwight D. Eisenhower and his wife Mamie. And here I am stringing together car batteries and tin cans.

Okay.

See the effect and not the source. In the beginning my motto was a necessity, not an aesthetic decision. You didn't know that, did you?

I hid the fixtures and lit up the palm trees. The effect was fantastic. The client, media magnate Walter Annenberg, loved it so much he introduced me to the Eisenhowers, who had both admired it. In fact, the president and first lady loved it so much they immediately ordered a similar set-up for their vacation.

And this, as you might guess, is when my hobby (low-voltage, soft outdoor lighting) got out of hand.

It's funny, looking back on it. I don't think I could have gotten away with anything like that today. Someone would have taken a look at my planning stage, seen a litter of tin cans and mayonnaise jars, and immediately notified the Secret Service, who surely would have decided I was crazy, perhaps hiding a homemade time bomb in one of these crazy things. I never could have done it. But things were different then, and this was enough to get me and my hobby up off the ground.

My lighting for the special event at the Eisenhower vacation retreat also went over well, making an impression on a number of politicians, foreign dignitaries, and all manner of socialites. *Mañana* was getting closer all the time.

Some of my early work in Washington, D.C.

This kicked off a long, interesting string of jobs for sitting presidents. I worked closely with Lady Bird Johnson and the capitol landscape architect, showing the latter some of the possibilities of 12-V lighting. Around this time I also had the distinctly unique experience of watching the president's two young daughters, Lynda and Lucy, come down into the basement kitchen for some breakfast—sleepy-eyed, their hair in rollers, still wearing night shorts—and being literally pushed out of the way by the White House staff, who were in the midst of assembling a state luncheon.

Rough way to grow up, I thought then (and still think today).

My association with the capitol architect led to an invitation to light President Nixon's "Western White House" in San Clemente, California. This building was very unpretentious, an H-shaped facility. On one side was the service wing, on the other was the sleeping wing, and in the middle was the living and working area.

Western White House, with Nightscaping

The Western White House sat on a 75-foot-high bluff overlooking the ocean. What a gorgeous view that was. Still, it reinforced my already strong sense of how much we citizens isolate our presidents, forcing them to live completely apart in the name of security. I observed President Nixon and his wife Pat retiring to their bedroom, which opened onto an interior courtyard, with a Secret Service man standing right on the other side of it all night. I observed them sitting on one of the benches overlooking the ocean, trying to watch the sunset, with Secret Service agents always within earshot. I observed the lack of privacy—the inability of two people to tell each other what they were really thinking without filtering it.

All of this made me feel rather grateful to be merely lighting the homes of the presidents. I never could have made it as one. (Of course the privacy and isolation issue isn't the only reason, but it's the one I like to focus on.)

It's a good lesson on being careful what you wish for. A lot of people just starting out seem to have a fairly vague, clouded notion of what success is and what they want from it. An outcome that might feel like success to one person (the presidency) might feel like prison to another (anyone who hates losing every last shred of their privacy).

I find that most young entrepreneurs simply define success as a future where money pours down from the heavens and everyone is smiling. Well, they get older, and most people shape their idea of success a little more clearly. Freedom to pursue their interests, a job where they can influence people or use their talents to the maximum. A comfortable lifestyle for their families, certainly a lack of want. An easy retirement. World travel. The luxury of being their own boss.

The logo of my El Camino ranch

No matter what kind of success you're after, it's important to define it. Try to get beyond the usual definitions and really figure out what it means to you. What will money do for you, besides the obvious? What kind of non-monetary indicators of success can you identify? Knowing exactly what you're after makes the pursuit that much easier. It makes the decision-making process, in many cases, clearer and more simple.

Knowing what your idea of success is also involves knowing what it excludes. Does your idea of success involve working 14-hour days at age fifty? Does it involve responsibility for hundreds, perhaps thousands, of employees and their livelihoods? Does it involve social responsibility or local involvement?

For me it sure felt like success when I installed my Nightscaping system in Mrs. Nixon's Rose Garden. A great experience, a true honor—these kinds of achievements are right up there in my personal definition of success.

After I installed the lights, by the way, the Secret Service needed to test them. Make sure they were secure, effective, all that. How did they do this, you ask? With the fancy light meters and high-tech spy equipment they certainly had at their disposal?

Not at all. They used a cat.

Once it got dark the agents let the Nixon's gray cat loose in the Rose Garden. Their reasoning was that if they could see the cat everywhere it ran, anywhere in the garden, and if they could still see one another in their dark coats, then the lighting system was adequate. Suffice to say, the lighting system passed.

Again it was a matter of the effect, not the source.

I still have goals, elements of success I've not yet achieved. Not all of them, of course, have to do with business. I believe everyone needs to, well, have a life. If you're focused on nothing but business your whole life, you're definitely going to miss out on the best parts. This advice is nothing new, but it bears repeating.

Part of my creed is that a person must have an overriding goal, something to drive them through the days. This can and should change as one goes through life. For a long, long time my goal was to see the year 2000. Well, it came and went. I was nearly 80 years old. What to do now?

I moped around for almost a year without a goal, having nothing to look forward to in that big sense. Then I hit upon an idea.

I liked then, and still do, to ride my bicycle around the bike trails of Palm Springs, with their beautiful scenery and many opportunities for people-watching. So I decided that for my 100th birthday I'd throw a huge party, invite my friends from all over the world to come ride down the main street of Palm Springs on their bicycles.

Soon I was excited again. What a party that will be! You're all invited to come, too. The only rule is that you must bring your bicycle and ride down that street with us.

In my version of success, nobody gets to be an observer.

Concepts

- Building and maintaining a successful business requires a **delicate balance between planning for the future and meeting the exigencies of the day.**

- **The ability to envision the future** is *the* key trait of a successful entrepreneur and the common denominator of those who achieve the most.

- **A lack of patience**, in terms of expecting huge and immediate success, **can derail your enterprise** before it even gets off the ground. (By leading you, for instance, toward high anxiety and bad decisions.)

- **Don't get caught up in the myth of the "runaway business."** The impossible majority of businesses take years to grow, and some take that long to even show a profit.

- **Expect obstacles.** A good chunk of each day should be spent planning for contingencies, reexamining current needs in the full light of *mañana*.

- The idea of *mañana*, defined by me as looking to the future with optimism, can **help ground your day-to-day operations**, while at the same time creating a good framework for growth.

- Conversely, by pouring yourself into every detail of the moment, you'll **help secure the future of your business.**

- It's important to **define your own personal ideas of success**, and do this in the clearest manner possible. These definitions will, in the end, function as a sort of guidance system when you're faced with tough decisions.

- I believe in a **goal-oriented life** and strongly encourage you to set a number of goals for yourself concerning the short-, mid- and long-term. Revisit them every year, and change, invent, and adjust as your ideas develop or your goals are met.

10 Reflection Questions

1. How adept are you at envisioning the future? (I'm not talking about Nostradamus-type predictions here, but merely the ability to follow a diverse set of cause-and-effect relations down the chain.)

2. In what ways could you imagine improving your skill at this necessary practice of entrepreneurship? What type of scaled systems could you practice with?

3. Do you consider yourself a patient person? What are your expectations for the first sixth months of your business venture? The first year? The five or ten after that?

4. Are you more of "live in the moment" or "forward-looking"? Do you feel able to balance these two often rival impulses?

5. Are your ideas of success based mostly on money or do they include many different spheres of life? Can you name five things a successful business would do for you, beside providing an income?

6. Do you have a concrete set of goals in both business and life?

7. How have your goals changed over the past five years? Can you use this information to predict what you'll be interested in five years from now?

8. How do you rate your own tenacity—more specifically, your ability to survive in tough circumstances with reward still on a rather distant horizon?

9. Review your current plans for your business carefully. Is your scheme at all infected by vagueness arising from the myth of the runaway business?

10. What common trappings of success are *excluded* from your own personal definition?

Chapter 6

Make Friends . . . . a Lot of Friends

My Story

Much of what life is about, in my opinion, has to do with human connections. Most specifically, the relationships you form with the group known as "friends and family." Life as I know it is bound up inextricably with these relations. And I've found them to be as important in business as they are in the other spheres of life.

You always need someone to help you when you're starting out. That's an ancient and unchanging truth. To paraphrase the old saying, "There was never a young person who succeeded in this world without attracting the interest and help of an older person."

Business relationships don't necessary need to be between the young and old to be beneficial, of course. The point here is that without befriending someone who knows what they're doing—an "insider," if you will—your task will be almost impossible.

What's more, as all businesspeople have learned, without developing a large network of contacts and friends, you'll have little chance of sustaining your business through the toughest time. It's very import to maintain good relationships. Why is this?

Because something will inevitably go wrong in your business, because you will, at some point, need to go somewhere for help, with goodwill your only bargaining chip. Forming strong bonds early is similar, in some ways, to creating a second family, one that will nurture you and ultimately protect you when you're down. More than this, your network will also be a boon under relatively clear skies, providing valuable information, counsel, references, etc. A fair—and foul-weather friend, indeed.

And what's the price of all this? Some of your time. Some of your sympathy and attention. A few smiles, handshakes, and well-considered words. For this you'll receive real friendship, in addition to the aforementioned boost to your enterprise. Of course you'll be expected to show the same consideration to your friends when they're in need as they show to you. That's the nature of friendship, after all.

For many people, this chapter will come as no surprise. People drawn to the business lifestyle are often gregarious by nature, and making friends is often a lesson learned early in any kind of business setting—educational or professional. Still, a surprising number of young people today either take this dictum lightly or disregard it entirely, perhaps seeing it as a relic of cronyism, of pre-Information-Age business. They believe, from my experience, that many of the old rules of business no longer apply.

Certainly, that's partly true. I write this in a much different era than the one I came of age in. In fact, I came up two or three eras ago. Things have changed, and I'm not about to dispute that, or state that the rules of business are timeless. The one under discussion, however, is about as close as they come. Trying to succeed in running your own business while neglecting, at the same time, to build a network of friends associated with your industry is like taking outfitting a ship with a crew, taking on precious cargo, arranging for a buyer in a foreign land, and then taking the most dangerous, difficult, stormy, and isolated route possible, rather than navigating through well-traveled, well-populated shipping channels. Encounter trouble in the first case, and you're lost, on your own. On the other hand, in the second case you'll have people around to fish you out of the water, save your crew, and perhaps even salvage the cargo and ship.

In less dire circumstances—to stay with the ship metaphor for a moment—friends help you when you've navigating unfamiliar waters. They can get you back on course before the whole voyage is lost. Again, this is as true in life as it is in business. As an example, I'd like to talk about a story from my late childhood, one I'm not particularly proud of, but which certainly helped set me on the right course, and which I still look back to today as a seminal moment in my development.

In my youth, when I was 13, 14, or thereabouts, I was prone to thinking things were mine that didn't belong to me. Late one night I was out searching for these type of items when I found a big Buick touring car parked outside a house. Voila.

After a few minutes I had the left rear wheel almost off the thing. Just then a man emerged from the house, which was about the last thing I'd expected at that hour. Before I knew it he had me by the collar. Luckily (unluckily, I thought at first), I'd been "borrowing" the back wheel of the one doctor in town, who at that moment was going off on an emergency call. Somewhere a woman was about to die.

Under these circumstances the man didn't have time to deal with me. He went off to burrow a neighbor's car, letting me know as he went that he expected the wheel to be back on his car when he returned later that night. Suffice to say, I reattached it and got out of there as quick as I could.

For several months after that, I successfully dodged the town doctor. I was careful to not see him, and doubly careful not to let him see me. But, as we all know, these kinds of strategies eventually fail in small towns (they generally also fail in medium-sized ones—and even big ones. Life is just that way). Though I'd absorbed some of the lesson of that fateful evening—surely, if another car hadn't been available for the doctor, I could have stood in the way of someone's life being saved—it took a second meeting with the doctor for the full lesson to be revealed.

One day when rounding a corner downtown, I ran smack into him. There he was, face to face with me, just like a bad dream.

"I've been looking for you, son," he said.

I knew he'd been looking for me, though I was smart enough not to reply with something like, *That's funny, Doc, because I've been running away from you.* I simply gaped up at him, wondering what would happen next. Police? A thrashing? Public humiliation? All three?

Yet the doctor didn't seem angry as he stood there, looking down at me. So maybe I wasn't as surprised as I might have been with the words that followed.

"I need someone to take care of the lawn in back of my office," he said. "I'll pay you two dollars per week."

All of a sudden I had a job. An income. What's more, shortly thereafter the doctor referred me to the pastor of the local Presbyterian church, where I was allowed to help the janitor for five dollars a week. Not bad money for a kid in those days.

And this was the end of my mistaking other people's property for my own.

Without the friendship and goodwill of that doctor, I probably wouldn't be where I am today. Which is why I try to pass it on whenever I can. These kinds of positive acts cannot go unrewarded, in my opinion. Which is why I stress that the most important part of making friends in business is *being a friend*, and a good one, to whomever you might come across. As many a wise person knows, kind acts tend to feed off one another.

Another lesson in this came to me years later, when I was married and traveling the country with a wife and two small daughters. We'd made it all the way across the country in our 30-foot trailer home, all they way to Bergen, New Jersey. One day my youngest daughter came home from school and announced that since she knew everyone in school it was time for us to move. My wife and I laughed, but she was learning the lessons of the road well, and we obliged her.

This brought about our trip down to Birmingham, Alabama to work on a project of which I'd learned. It was on this trip that we met the traffic trout-fisherman mentioned earlier in the book. This was not, however, the only learning experience of the drive.

It's to my great embarrassment that I admit trying to stretch my luck on one leg of the trip, running out of gas a long way from nothing. So there we were, miserable and stranded by the side of the road. It wasn't like today, with the cell phones and onboard tracking systems that keep you connected to everyone all the time. This was not a great situation to be in for anyone, let alone a man with a wife and two young daughters.

Before I even could begin to figure out what to do next, however, a fellow passing in a pickup truck stopped, got out of his vehicle, and asked us what the problem was. Once he understood our predicament, he smiled and went to the back of his pickup truck, coming back with a container filled with what looked liked gas.

"Here," he said. "I have this five-gallon can of gas." He stopped me before I could protest or offer to pay him. "It's free. I got it that way, so you pass it on."

Then he got back in his pickup truck and drove away.

I never saw this man again, but after I put some gas in our grateful tank and got out of there, I followed his instructions. Several states later I happened on the same situation and passed on the full can. Can you imagine the smile that comes out on people's faces when you hand over a five-gallon can of gas? It's reward in itself, I can tell you that.

Three months later I was sitting at a service station in yet another state, and a man came in with an identical gas can, saying he needed to fill it because someone down the road had just given it to him. I smiled to myself and understood once again the old maxim, *What goes around, comes around.*

I still believe that—even when my stabs at friendship or kindness in my business life end badly. Do I have examples of that? Most certainly.

Perhaps the most costly case of a business friendship gone wrong occurred in the late 1950s, soon after the Cuban revolution. Our church volunteered to take in some of the families exiled. One of the young men belonging to one of these families had been a practicing attorney and a CPA in Cuba. So I took him on; he was truly sharp and a great help to me at the office.

I felt sorry for him and his family, forced to live so far from their homeland. I also felt sorry for his father, who was incarcerated in Cuba. At the time I was flying my own single-engine plane, a Navion Rangemaster. I agreed to help the young lad get money into Cuba.

This arrangement went on for some years. My new company, still in the first decade of its Eisenhower-inspired life, was growing. We'd sold stock and were doing well; I had a board of directors, the whole nine yards. As the fifties became the sixties, the future looked rosy.

Then one day, just before Christmas, the lad called in and said he was sick, wouldn't be in. No problem. Yet later that day, I opened one of the drawers in his desk to find something I needed, and by accident came across an absolutely shocking mess. A huge pile of unpaid bills, including a notice of withholding from the Internal Revenue Service (IRS) demanding immediate payment. I was completely floored.

I went first to check the bank account, which in my foolish trust I hadn't been keeping track of. There was barely anything there. Certainly not enough to pay off the IRS. Barely enough, in fact, to meet the next payroll.

Good times gone away.

Next I went down to see our friendly banker. I wasn't panicking, but I wasn't in the greatest mental place either. But surely there had to be some way out of this. It was like a big misunderstanding, though my crooked employee knew exactly what he was doing. Surely some of the institutions with which my business was involved would understand, would come to my rescue in some fashion or another?

With this in mind I sat in front of the desk of our friendly banker. As clearly as I could I explained the situation. Told him I needed a loan to help get me through the short term. He listened to me. He was friendly. He was sympathetic.

When I was done speaking he looked at me and said he was sorry. But he couldn't help me. I already had a loan out with them, after all. In fact, he told me, we're going to have to attach your account. For those scoring at home, *attach* means to seize someone's property. So even the little money in the account was no longer available.

Not a good situation in which to be. With my account attached and closed, the checks I had already put out, which included my payroll checks, were not honored. And, as any businessperson can tell you, putting out bad checks to creditors is not a terribly good advertisement for a company. Even worse, putting out bad paychecks invites mutiny and desertion.

Merry Christmas, Bill.

It didn't get any better after that, either. Early one morning, right after Christmas, a gentleman in an overcoat appeared at my office. He said he was from the IRS, and I had no reason to not believe him. This man said he was attaching *the company*. This is when I got a little dizzy, only now starting to truly realize I could lose everything I'd built over this. The IRS agent forced me to leave the office under his watch and locked the doors with me outside.

Well, that couldn't stand for long. A little while later I broke a window, came back in, and got back to business. As much business as I had left, anyway.

Locked out by the IRS

Though things were truly bleak at this point, this is when the help of a true business friend pulled me through the fire. Just in the nick of time, a very special stockholder of mine loaned me enough cash to satisfy the IRS and calm the local banker enough to get my operation rolling again. I've never forgotten this kindness and trust, which more than made up for the betrayal that had met my own.

And I believe things work like this in life, more often than not.

Yet I still wasn't completely clear. To continue operating I needed more cash. My board of directors suggested I go into factoring, or sell my invoices for less then they were worth to them, in order to fix my cash flow problem. This was the worst, nastiest piece of business I ran into with that ill-fated board—and one of the most vicious I've ever run into with anyone. All the incoming checks were now payable to them. They kept a percentage on everything, and it was three years before I was clear and rid of them.

Perhaps it would have been wiser to have gone into bankruptcy. Many people urged me to do this at the time, but I was too proud for it. Looking back, I can honestly say this is one time pride served me well, and that I'm glad I didn't do it.

It was this incident, perhaps, that made me so sensitive to businesspeople in trouble. Especially friends, people I'd worked with for a long time. I made a point of helping out whomever I could, in whatever way I could.

In my opinion friendship is the glue of American business, and a lot of this country's success has been built upon the more genial aspects of its marketplace. The cooperation and mutual kindnesses. Sure it can be nasty. But it can also be surprisingly nice, as long as you're willing to catch more flies with honey.

Many years ago one of my first distributors in north-central California had a tremendous fire at his warehouse. It was completely wiped out, along with about $700 worth of Nightscaping fixtures. Now, this was back when $700 meant a little something.

Neither the distributor nor I were in position to absorb that kind of loss. Yet his was much, much greater in its totality. From my experience with the IRS and factoring I knew what he was facing. Without even thinking much about it I replaced at no charge all the inventory he'd acquired from us. I wanted to do what I could to save his business from ruin.

Though I couldn't foresee it then, that gesture of friendship resulted in several million dollars' worth of sales for Nightscaping in subsequent decades. Despite what people tell you, most kind acts don't go unrewarded.

I'm also a firm believer in the sharing of information and knowledge. You meet a lot of very strange people out there who are ultra-secretive about everything they do, as if every idea they have is worth a gold brick. I'm not so confident in my genius. Instead I simply try to pass on whatever I've learned that may be of use to another person.

I believe this style has won me friends and reaped benefits for my business as well. It's also made me feel like I'm doing all I can to help other people. And pay back my debt to God, which I believe is large, and getting larger every day I live.

One result of my attitude toward openly sharing information between friends resulted in "NIGHTchat," an interactive email program that connects me to over 500 contractors who use our products. In this forum we exchange all sorts of knowledge: things we've all learned about design, sales, installation, safety—all the aspects of Nightscaping that are vital to the independent businesspeople who install our fixtures.

Another rewarding experience, one of the most rewarding I've ever had, involved teaching a group of high school students how to form and operate a business. I did this with a friend of mine, a local optometrist, and our friendship made it an even more special experience. I tried to give the students the best fruits of my knowledge, teaching them about the necessities of profit, that everything depends on it, and that hard work alone won't guarantee a successful business. I told them you also need to recognize breaks when they come, that you need to have the courage to take advantage of them.

And I told them about the importance of making friends.

Concepts

- **The importance of making friends** is one of the first lessons most people learn in the world of business, and it's also among the most crucial.

- This idea includes **developing a network of friends and associates in your industry.** This group should be enlarged, maintained, and strengthened throughout your business career. Outside of your own initiative, they will be your most important assets.

- It's nearly impossible to get a leg up without **some kind of help from a more established or savvy friend**. In other words, seek out and treasure the mentor relationship.

- Trying to navigate the shoals and shallows of the marketplace **without friends is a dangerous and ultimately low-percentage strategy**.

- **Invest the relatively small amount of time necessary to nurture your business relationships**. They will often pay you back many times over. (And it's worth it to remember real friendships can be fun and rewarding outside the sphere of business as well.)

- Our company motto, one that's served us well for more than 40 years, is **"Friends Doing Business with Friends."** In my opinion every potential entrepreneur would benefit from meditating for a moment on this phrase.

- Even though you may eventually be burned in a business friendship or offer a hand to someone who bites it, you shouldn't let it sour you. Remember, it's as true in business as it is in life: *What goes around, comes around.*

- **Pass on whatever you can give, including knowledge and information**. Your generosity will not go unnoticed and will very often return be returned to you when you're in need.

10 Reflection Questions

1. How are you at building and maintaining friendships in everyday life? Do you see yourself more as a gregarious person or a loner? (Both can succeed in business, of course, though those given to solitude will often find the demands of running a company intolerable after a while.)

2. Do you treat people differently in your working life? Do you tend to value coworkers or other people you meet in a professional sense less or more than friends you meet in the outside world? Why?

3. Are you the type who will stick around and chat in a random way with someone for ten minutes, or do you always feel like you're too busy?

4. Where does friendship fall on your list of priorities?

5. Are you more prone to open yourself to advice from others or practice a "go-it-alone" style? Which one, in your experience, bears more fruit?

6. Are you generous with knowledge and information you might gather, in terms of passing it along to people who may benefit from it? Or are you naturally tight-lipped? If the latter, why?

7. Do you tend to trust people or do you rarely "put your neck out"? If you fall into the second category, can you isolate an experience that might explain your reluctance to trust others?

8. Do you think people are generally selfish and only interested in their own gain, or do you believe that the majority is guided by a wish to be of use?

9. Do you see the human side of your business life—interaction with the people with whom you deal on a regular or semi-regular basis—as fulfilling in itself, or as a necessary evil?

10. Imagine you receive a call from two other business owners, both asking for help. They have the same problem, but you can help only one. One has always been short and functional in your dealings; the other is warm and personable, asking about and remembering details of your personal life. Whom are you most likely to help? Why?

Chapter 7

Get Involved in Your Local (and Non-Local) Communities

My Story

You've got to give before you can receive!

I truly believe this, contrary to the popular ideas out there today. One thing I've learned during my time on this earth, if nothing else, is that you need to "give something back," as the saying goes. People don't really seem to understand this anymore, so I'll do my best to explain what should be a relatively simple concept.

You gotta live somewhere. That's the truth. Even if you're not all that concerned about your fellow man, the well-being of others, and all that goes with it (and of course, most people reading this will be concerned), even if these thoughts don't influence you at all, you should want to improve the place in which you choose to reside. That's just common sense. If no one gets involved things will go downhill very fast, right before your eyes.

Even if this call to duty doesn't stir you, even if you say, "That's why they hire people to take care of things around here," then there's still at least one reason to get involved locally: it's good for business.

I know that in this age of the Internet, in this time where everything seems it's going online or is about to, people take the idea of localities very lightly. *What does it matter*, they ask, *whether I live in Des Moines or Dubai? It's all the same. And if it's all the same, why do I need to pay attention to getting involved locally?*

The answer is simple: your physical location is your base of operations. Your environment. And it's very important to squeeze every last possible drop of resources from your environment.

If you do business in the physical world, that is to say, offline, then the advantages of this should be obvious. You open a café, say—or a video shop. Put up a sign for tax help. Start a landscaping business. Your very next move should be to get out there and meet the people in your area, as many as you can. Do this by any means necessary. Public events, charity, community gatherings, etc. And if you find a shortage of these opportunities, well, the smart thing to do is create your own.

At their best, see, businesses create communities around them. Even the meanest enterprise binds a few souls together. This doesn't always fit into a strict local definition of community—our NIGHTchat email group, for instance, encompasses more than 500 Nightscaping contractors from all across the country. This, surely, is a community.

So for the examples given above, the choices are rather obvious. Opened a café or a video store? Then get reading groups or live music into the former. Start a movie club for the latter, with associated discounts and events that draw on your knowledge. For the other examples the ideas are the same. Run regular tax-help seminars. Get gardening or landscaping clubs together—forums where you can display your skills and let people with similar interests spread the word.

Of course those with charitable or volunteering instincts will see more opportunities and have reasons for getting involved which lay beyond business needs. Donating some of your time to local schools, charitable organizations, civic groups, and even governmental functions will both satisfy the giver in you and further the interests of your enterprise, though the latter will be a secondary concern to this group.

Even if, in the beginning, your primary concern is your fledgling business, you will be surprised. Civic work can be a reward in itself, and the feeling of completeness it engenders can be addicting. Getting involved locally, giving back to the community, actually improving the place in which you live—few activities are more satisfying as one grows older.

Even those whose primary place of business will be online—a sizable and ever-growing group these days—will benefit from some kind of local involvement. A number of websites begin as local phenomenon, for instance, and only later spread across the country. The classified service known as Craig's List comes to mind.

Another aspect of local involvement concerns the breaks you'll often receive as a valued member of a given community. Local governments both want and need more successful businesses in their jurisdiction. If you're seen as a boon to the community, very often you'll qualify for breaks and incentives that might be denied another business. Those who administer your town or district will often do what they can to help. This concept is very similar to the one discussed in the previous chapter, though here the idea is to make friends with *the community at large*.

By engaging with the community at large, you'll make connections that form part of your burgeoning support network, you'll meet individuals who will become your friends and allies, and you'll increase the exposure of your enterprise, which is almost always a desirable thing.

It took me a while to figure out where I wanted to put my roots down, but when I did, I went forward at full speed. I advise any burgeoning entrepreneurs to spend some time traveling, figuring out what areas of their region, their country, their world, suit them best. After all, it's much easier to get involved locally and stay interested if you actually like the people and place you're getting involved with.

After about three years traveling the continental United States with my wife and daughters, we all decided more or less together that it was time to return home to Southern California. With my wanderlust mostly taken care of by three long years on the road, I was ready to find a place to stay for a long time.

Redlands University, part of a beautiful place

Redlands, California happened to be this place. Not far from the Victorville train station in which I was abandoned; not far from Lucerne, where I'd ridden backwards on a burro through my boyhood; not far from the Hemet farm or from the Colton cement plant in which I'd first learned about electrical work. Yet still far enough that I didn't get too caught up in the old memories, which weren't all that great.

Redlands was known as a family-friendly place, a nice community in which to raise your kids and get old. The climate and air seemed good for my youngest daughter's asthma condition as well—those of many of the towns we'd been living in during our trip hadn't been so good. So, having found our place, now it was time for me to get going.

One of the first things I did was to buy an old, run-down orange grove. There was plenty of room here for my old Quonset hut, which had largely been collecting dust over the past three years. I moved it here to Redlands from Colton and started up again.

There were a ton of successful agricultural owners in the area, and it's in this field—large agricultural/industrial electrical systems—that I began to concentrate. Doing a good job was only one aspect of building a successful contracting business, however. Redlands was a very tight-knit community, and to get anywhere you had to become a part of it.

So I did. One of the most famous members of the Redlands community was the country singer "Tennessee" Ernie Ford. I had the privilege of meeting and getting to know Ernie, and before too long we started up the Kiwanis pancake breakfast, a local event that drew a lot of hungry folks on our weekly meeting date. These breakfasts were excellent opportunities for networking, both for me and for the people who came.

This is an important point—very often, these kinds of events can be beneficial to other people looking to network. If you provide a venue in which they can do so, your events will grow in popularity, and—provided your business itself is sound and necessary—you should do well.

The entrance to my "El Camino Ranch"

I didn't stop, however, with the Kiwanis pancake breakfast. As you'll remember, there was also the Redlands Bowl lighting gig, which I did for many years. What's more, I eventually joined the Redlands country club—another excellent networking opportunity—joined a city improvement committee in the Chamber of Commerce, and was an active member of the Boys and Girls Club. The latter was another good example of how you can help in ways that satisfy and reward you. If anyone knew about at-risk children it was me, who once could so easily have taken a permanent wrong turn.

All these experiences reinforced how important it is to network—how important it is to share. Share what? Yourself. What part of yourself? Your resources, your life, and your ideas. You do something like volunteer time at the Family Services association, and you meet some pretty influential people who will open doors for you.

I also made a point of becoming conversant in some of the more important local industries. This was important for my electrical business, but it also allowed me to talk the talk with some of the more successful owners in town.

Orange cultivation, for instance, was a major local source of revenue. I was interested in the agricultural industry, and, as the owner of a run-down orange grove, I had a good reason to be. I enrolled in some classes at the University of California-Riverside, learning about all aspects of the orange industry, from citrus propagation to tree care to disease control to marketing. Though I never became an orange baron, this training did allow me to speak the same language as the successful local growers, which helped my business immeasurably.

Thus being connected to and knowledgeable about a matter of extreme local importance contributed to my business in a major way.

As I said earlier, however, not all "communities" must necessarily be local. There are many different types of communities, some united by geography, other by interest, others by culture or background. I strongly believe that it's in any business owner's best interests to plug into as many communities as he possibly can.

One community that I was part of, and still am, is that of the electricians. I was a union contractor for a long time, as well as a member of the National Electrical Contractors Association (NECA). It was my union affiliation that allowed me to travel the United States, going from union hall to union hall, and getting work everywhere I went.

I was also a member of NECA's National Education Council. This was an excellent opportunity for me to spread the word, evangelize about the work I was doing in outdoor lighting. As I traveled to district meetings I brought with me one of my first prototype 12-V fixtures to show it to other contractors. This earned me a lot of strange looks.

But it was the beginning of my "hobby that got out of control," as I always put it to people who ask me how I began my business. I was truly interested in the product I was working on, and in the people with whom I was interacting. Sure, it wasn't easy. Very often I heard, *12-volt? What the hell is that?* Or *What a cute fixture . . . what do you do with it?* This taught me the value of one-on-one sharing, of overcoming objections, of stressing again and again the worth of your product in a larger community setting.

Concepts

- **Local or community involvement** is extremely important to any business, but is especially important to new ones.

- **Communities don't necessarily need to be local.** In fact, communities can be bound by many factors, only one of which is geographic. Common interests, profession, culture, and religion are some of the others. It's advisable to **become a part of as many communities as you can.**

- Local involvement will be **beneficial to many people on a personal level**, as a means of giving back. *You gotta give before you receive*, I always say.

- Even if you're not that interested in local involvement, you should still try for **some level of effective representation**, for exposure and networking purposes if nothing else. (Community involvement and civic life can be addicting, however, so don't surprised to see yourself going from apathetic to hooked.)

- Make sure the community in which you base your operations is one you enjoy! This sounds simple, but a surprising number of people don't give a whole lot of thought to environment. Obviously it's **much easier to get involved with people and a place that you connect with on a basic level**.

- **If there aren't many opportunities for local involvement in your area, you must create them**. This can involve starting local clubs or interest groups based around the good/services you provide, or free trials/seminars, or informational meetings, etc. etc. Ask yourself what your business provides that can help the local community.

- **Donations to children's or civic events or groups** are also a very positive method of local involvement and create a very good impression (some have likened it to advertising of a sort).

- Even those whose businesses are Internet-based or otherwise do most of their work non-locally should get involved and **present themselves as a boon to the community**, as this may bring extra consideration from important and decision-making locals at key junctures.

10 Reflection Questions

1. How involved are you now with the locality in which you live? Do you consider community service an important activity? How high on your list of priorities does it rank?

2. What type of communities, using some of the parameters we've already offered, are you a current or potential member of?

3. Do you find it more comfortable to join forces with a large group toward a common goal or to work on your own?

4. What advantages of heavy community involvement can you identify on your own? Can you think of any drawbacks?

5. Who, in your opinion, holds ultimate responsibility for the quality of the community? How much individual responsibility do citizens have?

6. What type of charities and civic organizations interest you? What types of problems or issues would you like to address, if you had the power, on a local level?

7. How much responsibility does a business have to the community in which it is based? What percentage of an entrepreneur's time should reasonably be devoted to local/community involvement in a given week?

8. If you were to search for opportunities for local involvement in your area, to which resources or media would you turn?

9. How important do you think local businesses are to civic life? How important do you think they should be?

10. Once you've identified non-local communities of which you're a potential member, how would you go about becoming a member? Once a member, how would you go about advancing your business interests?

Chapter 8

Understand Your Customers' Motivations

My Story

Why Light? This simple question has served me for years and years as a quick and easy reminder of why it is that I do what I do. It reminds me, through all the tough and indecisive moments, of my real objective: to please the customer.

Yet each time I have to think about it. *Why light?* is a question with many possible answers, and for each new client I'm forced to recalibrate my thinking. Every time, this question helps me focus like a laser on the specific individual for whom I'm designing a lighting display. *Why is this person installing outdoor lighting?*

For the party at Walter Annenberg's—the one where Dwight and Mamie Eisenhower admired my work and really got Nightscaping off the ground—I knew the occasion was to be a special one, so I really took care to light up every palm tree, to highlight each and every point of beauty visible on that man's property. I knew Annenberg wanted something spectacular, and that's exactly what I tried to give him.

For other clients the point isn't to create a spectacle. Many people don't want a huge light show blazing away on their property night after night. They want something quieter, more subdued. Something to pick up the subtler parts of their property—a path illuminated, a statue displayed against the darkness.

I knew how important it was to precisely gauge my clients' desires before spending a lot of time and money lighting up their property. The trick, I soon learned, was to gather this information without being annoying or obtrusive. People don't have time to answer a hundred questions or baby-sit you as you set up their systems. Sure, some people will micromanage, keep looking over your shoulder, and try to control every detail.

More often, however—especially if you have a good reputation—people give you a general idea, then tell you to go to it. Most people don't go into long, full-blown statements of why they're doing this and exactly what they want from it. As a result, very often you need to pick up subtle hints—little clues, perhaps, of what a husband and wife say. Discover some of their favorite aspects of the property, where they are most likely to focus their attention, etc. It's not a perfect business, but you've got to come as close as you can.

This is an exceptionally important part of entrepreneurship. You must anticipate your clients' needs, developing such skill at this that you know what they want even before they do. It may sound difficult, but eventually, mercifully, your clients begin separating into types. Then it's just a question of fine-tuning, looking to the small differences that set this particular person off from the others.

As I'll get into later in this chapter, my senses weren't always so keen. Like any young entrepreneur, I made costly mistakes. I must say, though, that each mistake brought me new knowledge, serving as what they call a "teaching moment." I urge you to see missteps in the same way—not as failures, but as opportunities to gain information or skills you've been lacking.

On the other hand, if you neglect the learning process inherent in mistakes, you're almost certainly bound for a short career as an entrepreneur. There's an ancient saying that explains three different kinds of horses. One, the worst, doesn't react until the whip lands on his back. The average horse reacts just before the whip strikes. The best horse, however, reacts to the rider even before the whip is raised.

It's good to be the best kind of horse in business. If you're really on, you'll be able to anticipate your clients' needs, initiating communication before they need to, and covering all possible angles. This is, as a matter of fact, the sign of a true professional.

Some businesspeople never quite get that it's the client that they're serving. They seem to attend to everything but the person standing in front of them. This is a very dangerous habit to indulge. It's one I received a lesson in quite early, long before I was involved with Nightscaping, even before I'd gone on my three year cross-country quest. It was in Colton, as a matter of fact. This was right after I'd set up my Quonset hut, with its little glassed-in retail space in the front. This was in the late 1940s, a time when portable electric heaters were just becoming popular. I decided to jump on the bandwagon and begin offering them to the customers who came to me in the morning and early evening, those hardy souls undeterred by the fact that my shop was only open a couple hours a day.

First I had to drive up to Los Angeles to attend a half-day teaching program on the devices, which were as new to me as anyone else. This class was put on by the manufacturers, who aimed to induce potential distributors to go ahead and start selling the line. Later on I would do the same with Nightscaping—educating contractors and landscapers became one of the most important parts of my job.

LITE-TIPS

Spotlighting News and Ideas in Landscape Lighting

April 1994   Volume 11, Number 10

Nightscaping University Attracts Variety

The afternoons were spent in this state-of-the-art classroom, where the "students" who had come from many different areas of the U.S. studied hard.

A good time was had by all at graduation night during the "Dutch Auction."

The partnership between NIGHTSCAPING and California Landscape Lighting created a very successful session of the Nightscaping University. The forty students were from California, and ten other states, representing electrical, irrigation, and landscape contractors as well as landscape architects. Our own President, Dave McWilliams, and Sales Managers Tony Susca and Herb Dizon also attended.

This varied group came together for 3½ days, March 5th through March 8th, to further their education in landscape lighting. Mornings were spent learning how to do night photography, and the afternoons contained lectures on design, engineering, and marketing. Each day, different aspects of these topics were covered, with a session on trouble-shooting towards the end. One of the most interesting parts of this "university" was the sharing of ideas, problems, and solutions of contractors from other parts of the country in a non-competitive environment.

The last evening was spent having dinner and "graduation." It was a fun evening which included a "Dutch Auction." A Nightscaping Demo Kit was awarded to winners Bill Conlon of C & S LANDSCAPE in Anaheim Hills, CA., Robert Davie of DAVIE LANDSCAPE in Sarasota, FL, and Bob Thornburg of ELECTRIC AID in Santa Fe, NM.

A few of the contractors stayed on an extra day to come up to Westlake Village and tour our facilities. They also met the entire CLL staff. During lunch, many of the contractors took advantage of our spring-like day and ate outside picnic style, which seemed to be the perfect end to their stay in sunny California. ■

CALIFORNIA LANDSCAPE LIGHTING

Article about Nightscaping "University"

I came back from the workshop excited, ready to sell the dickens out of these things. My very first customer came the next day. She was a little old retired Sunday-school teacher, a woman venturing out in the cold evening to my tiny shop. Apparently she'd read about these heaters and somehow learned I was selling them.

That was enough for me. Immediately I began talking up these heaters, telling her about all their specifications. About their great construction. *They're made of special wire. They won't tip over. They're safe and economical.* So on and so forth. I told her just about every great thing I'd learned about the heaters at the class the previous day. I made sure my pitch included every feature.

Finally, after all this, the woman looked up at me and asked a simple question.

"Bill, will this heater keep a little old lady warm?"

This was one of my first true lessons in sales. This woman didn't need to know the heater's specs. She didn't need to know about its wattage, its energy consumption, its special wire, or its failsafe mechanisms. She needed to know, very specifically, whether it would keep her warm at night.

Why light? Yes. And why is this kindly old lady in my shop? In my excitement I'd forgotten. I shook my head and had to grin. But I've never forgotten that exchange or the simple way the question was put to me.

Anticipating and responding to clients' wishes also played a part in the wiring jobs I would get around that same time. Wiring, admittedly, is a pretty easy sell—most people want it for the same reason: they need something electric to work. Not a lot of individualism there. Still, there were needs to be met.

My early contracting jobs often involved wiring houses for dryers. I'd been putting meters in tract houses for California Edison and some of these jobs were now bearing fruit. I got a lot of business from young fathers, in fact, who more than once came with a very particular request.

"Bill," they would say, "My wife's coming home from the hospital in two days and I need a dryer."

Well, this was the baby boom, and these young wives were going to the hospital and expecting to come home to a working electric clothes dryer, another novelty of the period. Women knew how much laundry they'd be doing with a new baby in the house. They wanted the newest, most modern way to deal with it all. But these dryers required wiring above and beyond what most people had in their homes, so they would call on me to do the upgrades. Two days before they were due.

I never did understand why the husbands, who knew they'd be needing a dryer for nine long months, would wait so long to call me. Well, I suppose I can kind of understand, being a man and all. Sometimes it's as if we think to ourselves, *Well, a meteor might fall on the house or something, so best to wait until it's time.*

In any case, these dryers needed to be wired up yesterday. As I was in need of customers for my fledgling contracting business and looking to please, I did my best to oblige. I didn't want, after all, a woman who'd just gone through labor to come home to no clothes dryer. Nor did I want these poor husbands to face any avoidable wrath.

I developed a nice store of goodwill through these rush jobs, and I learned during this time how important it was to provide the service when the customer wants it. Unless you're in a "necessity business," such as air-conditioner repair or plumbing, one thing you need to realize is that the client's timeframe is all-important. This is especially true for younger entrepreneurs, who are attempting to gain a slice of the market even though they're an unknown quantity—something most customers don't like to deal with.

In fact, no matter what business you're in, it's the client's happiness that should be your main objective. Forget about agreements, expectations, etc. Forget about your own issues or all the things you know that the client doesn't concerning how hard it is just to do your job. Your sole purpose, as an entrepreneur, is to make the person who's turning over a portion of her hard-earned money to you happy.

Otherwise you won't find many people willing to do it.

Promise less, produce more. That's another one of my tried-and-true mottos, with which you're no doubt becoming very familiar with by now. It may seem like a bit of a paradox at first, but the successful entrepreneur is extremely careful to avoid "promising the moon." Otherwise you'll end up disappointing people more often than not. So be cautious when you're pitching yourself. The temptation is to go overboard in hopes of getting a crucial early sale. Don't succumb.

Why? Your product or service should be enough to carry the day. If you are skilled at what you do, if you are selling something truly useful, then you don't need to "oversell." Just present your case plainly and honestly, then surpass the modest expectations you've set up.

Once you're truly skilled at dealing with clients, once you've developed a solid reputation, you'll acquire a sharp sense of how much "selling" you can and need to do with each individual. In the beginning, however, its best to remain low-key and refrain from telling anyone your product/service is going to change their life. Credulous people will be disappointed, and the shrewd will put up their guard at any hint of an oversell.

Just the same, even if you do everything right, you'll still end up with disgruntled customers. My best advice is to try to soothe every single customer you possibly can. Sure, there will be some maniacs and misanthropes who hate it no matter what you do. They're a part of business, and the best you can do with these folks is to learn to avoid them. However, when a reasonable customer is truly disappointed, most self-respecting entrepreneurs will do something to make amends. Leaving people truly unhappy with your work or product is an excellent way to put yourself out of business.

One of the interesting lighting projects I had early on, in the beginning of my career, was at the home of a very successful local agricultural owner. The man called me one day, having heard from someone or other, possibly myself, about my dabbling in the field of outdoor lighting. He told me he and his wife would be gone for a month on vacation, then asked if I would come and install a system in his backyard.

At this point I was eagerly taking all the lighting jobs I could, and I quickly agreed.

We said nothing about price. Since I'd dealt with him pretty extensively while doing jobs for his business, I wasn't particularly worried about being paid. These were the types of folks who, if you did a good job that pleased them, didn't quibble a whole lot as long as the price was within reason. Which is why I enjoyed working for them.

The man's home was about three hours away, and soon after our conversation I took a drive over to see what the layout was like. The owner and his wife were already gone on their month-long trip. I walked around the property and took some mental notes, trying to figure out some rough outlines of what I would do with it. I was looking for a center, something to base the lighting design around. These types of objects or areas usually popped up naturally. They were very visible. Once you saw it you said, *Okay, here's what we'll start with. Here's our highlight.*

Sure enough, in the far-right corner of the backyard I soon stumbled across something—the perfect center for a lighting display. It was a beautiful statue of a boy riding a dolphin, a gorgeous life-sized work. My young family and I had just seen the film *Boy on a Dolphin*, which starred a young Sophia Lauren as a Greek sponge diver who discovers a submerged statue of a boy riding a dolphin—a mystical artifact said to grant wishes. A fun film for all, it made this discovery a neat little coincidence; highlighting the piece just seemed natural.

Little did I know how much of a disturbance this happy coincidence would create.

I subsequently did the installation, making the boy and his dolphin the focal point. To this day I still consider it one of the finest designs and installations I've ever done. I was proud of my work and excited for the man and his wife to come home and see it.

The month passed quickly. Then one night about ten o'clock I get a call from the owner. It didn't take me one minute to realize how unhappy he was. Without learning of what the trouble was, I agreed to meet him at six o'clock the next morning to try and fix it.

The next morning at six AM sharp the homeowner met me by the front gate. Without much of a pause, he proceeded to tell me exactly what the trouble was. As it turns out, the dolphin statue had been given to him by his mother-in-law, whom he thoroughly detested. So having it as the glowing center of his backyard at night did not make him very happy.

In fact, there was another statue he'd wanted emphasized, a waterfall figure in the middle of the yard. I didn't think it was as nice as the other, though it was still beautiful. I'd kept it in the background of my lighting scheme. A mistake.

This statue turned out to be much loved by the man. He and his wife had been traveling though the South some months earlier and happened upon an old plantation being torn down. They discovered upon the grounds this waterfall figure, bought it, and had it shipped to California. In the process an arm had been broken off the figure, he explained to me. The statue was already so dear to him that he actually recruited a stone mason from Vermont to reattach the arm. It was his love, he said.

Well, I didn't need to hear much more than that. In my ignorance I'd made the hated mother-in-law statue the shining star of my design, while leaving the man's pride and joy in darkness. Now his upset manner on the phone the previous night made sense.

Immediately I set to work, removing the lighting from the boy and dolphin statue and redeploying it to the waterfall figure. Once I finished, the man paid the bill right away and afterward professed himself exceedingly happy with my work.

This is when I really woke up, I suppose, and figured out exactly how important the question of *Why light?* really is. After this episode I would be even more careful to gauge the desires, loves, and intense dislikes, of my clients. I realized that just by taking a simple walk around the grounds with the man and his wife, I would have been able to understand them and avoid the mistake I ended up making.

Luckily my error was easy to fix and didn't harm the project in the end. But it easily could have concerned something more permanent, in which case it would have damaged my working relationship with this man and quite possibly my reputation as well.

There are many, many such sinkholes waiting for the young entrepreneur. The world of clients and customers is vast and slippery. People's desires are as various as their faces. It's absolutely essential to understand them, for, as you navigate what can be a very dark and bewildering marketplace, they will often serve as your only light.

Concepts

- **Understanding client/customer motivations** is a key element of entrepreneurial success—the power of which cannot, in my opinion, be underestimated.

- It's crucial for those with fledgling businesses to **interpret, and focus, on the wishes of those whom they serve.**

- It's easy to get lost in the vagaries of business-school formulas or product specifications, but in the end it all comes down to one thing: **is the client/customer happy or not?**

- For my specific business, the question *Why light?* has always served as a means of **focusing my mind on the individual at hand**, recalibrating my thinking for their unique wishes and needs. I would urge young entrepreneurs to develop a similar reminder, some way of getting down to the most important aspects of each new project/product.

- One way to help ensure client satisfaction is to always **promise less, produce more.** The simple idea gives you a good chance to impress and delight, rather than disappoint, your client. Expectations exert a heavy psychological influence; only by managing them properly will you achieve your goal of customer satisfaction.

- It's essential to **anticipate your client's wishes.** That is, in terms of our horse-racing analogy, to move before the "whip" is raised.

- Though some people will have more natural ability than others in the arena of anticipation, this is a skill to be developed, **a combination of experience** with your own business **and the fine art of reading people.**

- **Better to clarify or ask questions of your client/customer** than to assume, out of pride or laziness, that you know exactly what they want. Confusing your ideas with those of your clients—as I did with the boy and dolphin statue—is a good way to get tripped up or put into an unpleasant situation.

10 Reflection Questions

1. How sensitive are you to the motivations of others? Are you a good "reader of people" or do you have trouble deciphering what people want without it being spelled out for you?

2. In what aspects of this could you see yourself improving, and through what means could you do so?

3. When you think about your business, do you see it mainly as a way to make money hand over fist, or as a genuine service to other people?

4. How good are you at listening? Do you tend to force your interpretations onto other people—or do you hear them out, listen to what they have to say, and then take it into consideration, acting accordingly?

5. In business situations do you ever put yourself in the place of the person with whom you're dealing?

6. What, in your mind, is more important—doing the job "right" as ordered or satisfying the customer? If these two elements conflict on a certain job, how would you handle it?

7. Can you identify any tendencies in yourself to talk things up too much, hyping them until they're inevitably a disappointment when they arrive?

8. What do you think is the proper balance between "selling" and "hyping"? Can you think of ways to sell people on your goods or services without hyping?

9. How willing are you to go the extra mile with your clients and customers, in terms of identifying their real needs and wishes? Have you ever dealt with a salesperson or service provider who assumed he knew, better than you did, exactly what you wanted and needed?

10. At what point do you think it's correct to say, "Okay, I've done enough, and I can't do any more," in regards to an unhappy customer? How far down the line should one go?

Chapter 9

Watch Out for Professional Advice (and Conventional Wisdom)

My Story

The path each successful business takes to profitability is completely its own. As with snowflakes, no two are alike. Thus what works for one business will often prove disastrous for another. It's for this reason, and a few others we'll touch on in a moment, that you should be very, very careful when a friendly soul takes it upon himself to give you some professional advice.

You should be even more careful with the body of ill-fitting garments known as conventional wisdom, which may in part apply to some enterprises, but, taken together, fit none of them well or completely.

I've come up through the business world the hard way—by creating my own company and suffering with it through all its failures and "fraying rope" moments. Of course, in more than 40 years in business, I've received enough advice of one sort or another to drown an elephant. When things are going wrong, when things are going well, when things are flatter than a pancake on Jupiter, or whenever big decisions need to made, you can be sure there will be dozens of people around to tell you just what you should do next.

Now, I really want to make something clear—I've received wonderful advice and guidance from friends over the years. There are a lot of people I've depended on at one point or another for counsel. On the other hand, there are some people who dispense advice like Pez and seem to worry little about whether or not you're interested in hearing it. One thing I've learned: some of the wisest people seem to understand the maxim that unsolicited advice is a form of hostility. Thus many people who "know" won't tell you unless you directly seek out their advice.

So I guess I'm saying beware the friend or associate who always seems to be indiscriminately spitting out advice. It's a lot of mental noise in the end and very likely won't do anything but confuse you.

The bevy of differing, conflicting opinions you'll encounter every day are one of the main reasons you should always get yourself clear on important matters as quickly as possible. Wavering is a horrible business practice and an utter waste of time. I'm not saying you shouldn't think about big decisions for a while—I'm saying you'll want to keep your own counsel and figure out what *you* think before hearing what ten other people think about it.

Once you know your own mind, it's much easier to sort through other people's points of view. If you're unsettled in your own thinking, however, you'll soon discover that all the advice starts rattling around and confusing you pretty quick. In other words, it's easy to get lost in other people's ideas. Better to trust your own instincts, which are usually well-matched to the exigencies of your business and its specific needs. Don't know why it happens that way, exactly, but it just does.

Conventional wisdom is a horse of a slightly different color. Sure, it can and often will come from the mouths of those giving you advice. But it's also out there in many other forms, waiting to invade your decision-making process. It comes from TV, film, books, and from yourself, in the form of a little voice inside your head that criticizes all but the safest choices.

Conventional wisdom is the voice of safety, the false religion of the masses. It's suffocating and often deadly to a business. Like cargo too heavy for a ship to bear, it will sink you slowly but surely. The trick is to start tossing it overboard as quickly as you can and continue doing so as long as you can.

When I think about the first years of my own business, there's nothing I can do but shake my head and smile. I made a lot of mistakes, simply put. Some of the worst ones involved professional advice and conventional wisdom.

My infamous board of directors, a group it took me years to rid myself of, was one example. But before I get into the details of that long fiasco, I suppose I should talk about the beginnings of my business itself.

Once the Eisenhowers had given me and my hobby a sheen of success and a running start, I began thinking more seriously about moving out of the electrical contracting business and into the production, installation, and selling of my 12-V system and fixtures. In the wake of the glamorous brush with the rich and powerful, it had become obvious that there was the possibility of a nice business here.

So, with a dear friend of mine, Howard Ranney, I established Loran. This was in 1959. Howard had just returned from military service and had served in the most recent war. He was on board with my idea. So he put up $200 and I put up $200, and the company that owns the buildings I'm sitting in right now was born.

LORAN – Redlands, California
P.O. Box 911   Telephone 793-2881 (Area Code 714)

CATALOG NUMBER AND PRICE SHEET

Nightscaping by LORAN — Flowers, Entrances, Shrubs, Trees, Fountains, Walks, Dining Areas, Planter Areas, Etc.

		Suggested List	Dealer
9"Hx2"W — Black — Brass Trim — LO-1073 lamp **LOCATOR** No. GU-0902-1		11.40	6.84
9"Hx5"W — Black — Brass Trim — LO-93 lamp **NAVIGATOR** No. GD-0905-1		13.75	8.25
26"Hx12"W — Black — Brass Trim — LO-1073 lamp **ILLUMINATOR** No. GD-2612-1		17.20	10.32
25"Hx10"W — Black — Brass Trim — LO-1141 lamp **DIRECTOR** No. GD-2510-1		15.95	9.57
4"Hx12"W — Black — Brass Trim — LO-1073 lamp **SPECTATOR** No. TD-0412-1		15.75	9.45
V-12 Transformers, non raintite 115V primary 12V secondary			
V12-637-401-25VA capacity 1-2 fixt.		7.40	4.90
V12-637-461-50VA capacity 1-4 fixt.		9.20	6.10
V12-637-471-100VA capacity 1-8 fixt.		13.40	8.85
V12-637-481-150VA capacity 1-12 fixt.		16.20	10.75
V12-100A—Approved Raintite		26.50	18.75
No. 12-2-100 UF Cable		10.00	8.50
No. 12-2- 50 UF Cable		5.00	4.25
2612 Shield		2.00	1.20
12 Volt Lamps			
LO-93		.35	.25
LO-1141		.35	.25
LO-1073		.35	.25

LORAN fixtures are individually packaged with a complete fixture in each carton. Fixtures are designed to operate on 12 volts A.C. LORAN fixtures are stock items, available through your Electrical Distributor.

Prices, finishes and manufacturing details subject to change without notice.

All items guaranteed for one year against manufacturing defects.

Freight allowed 100 pounds or more (approximately 50 units)

Terms 1% 10th prox.

Early Loran price sheet

We came upon the name *Loran* by combining our last names. I don't remember if it was intended to or not, but it ended up being at least a semi-shrewd move, bringing us some instant recognition, as an air-and-sea navigational system known as LORAN had been used extensively by the US in World War II and Korea, subsequently becoming very well-known and popular.

Thus we had no problem walking into the office of any young architect: I would simply say I was from Loran, and the man would perk up and say, "Okay, I've heard of that." Of course he would very often be fairly puzzled about what someone representing an air-and-sea navigational system could possibly have to say in his office.

Then I would explain it to him, trying to tell as much as I could about our 12-V outdoor lighting in the brief time before his eyes glazed over. And the usual response?

"Twelve volt? What the hell is that?"

It was a long road indeed.

Six months after the formation of Loran, Howard decided there were just too many people here in Southern California. The man sold his folks' orange operation and moved up to central California. I bought Howard's share of the business for $200 and was now the sole owner of a manufacturing company in its infancy.

In fact, it was still so much a baby that it was really just a hobby. I was making pretty good money and didn't depend on the nascent fixture business for any income. It was still just on the side. I believe anyone who can manage to keep their day job while running a new business should, by all means. It takes a lot of the stress and risk out of the endeavor. Letting a "hobby" mature into a real business is to me the smartest way to go about things. *Of course you do, Bill, because it's what you did!*

All professional advice aside, there will surely be many businesses and situations which won't allow the young entrepreneur to play both sides of the fence. So you just have to take the plunge. I didn't have to, exactly, though my business was precarious enough at times—during the Cuban accountant crisis, to cite one example. Every business will know a time of risk, it's axiomatic. Thus no entrepreneur will ever be spared the sickening dips of the roller coaster that is owning one's own business. The best you can do, I suppose, is inure yourself to it.

Well, back to the story. As my side business was looking fairly promising, and as I had a steady income from my contracting jobs, my all-wise accountant told me it was now time for me to go ahead and sell stock. Become a real corporation. So I did.

I sold stock for $1000 a share to friends and business associates only—no widows or orphans, I suppose. Very quickly I was sitting on $370,000—more money than I'd ever seen in my life. Seemed to take no time at all. Heady days, I must say.

So here I was with all this cash—and an operating budget. Along with it came a new entity, something I wasn't too familiar with: a board of directors. Turned out they had a little bit of power, and it wouldn't take long for me to figure this out. The board was composed of influential townspeople, local bigwigs who held any number of shares.

I was in tall clover, as they say, but it wouldn't last long.

For one thing, the board members had relatives. Many relatives. Spread out all over the country. And boy would they love a lighting system installed. At a cut-rate price. And I mean *cut-rate*. Funny, it wouldn't happen anymore these days, but all these folks expected I'd do this for them. And they were right. I had little choice.

The last thing I wanted to do was create a problem from the get-go with my powerful shareholders. So I went around doing these jobs, which not only robbed from the bottom line of the company, but also used up a great deal of my personal time.

So it goes. You sell pieces of your company, you sell pieces of yourself.

Around this time the board decided we needed some national exposure. Hmm. What to do? How about a full-page, four-color ad in *House Beautiful?* Perfect!

The ad cost $27,000. A nice chunk of the money I'd raised. And how many sales came out of this little piece of savvy professional advice? Not a single one.

Peoria Journal Star - Feb. 20, 1965

'Nightscaper' Impressed by City's Native Beauty, Area Topography

By C. VERNE BLOCL
Staff Writer

Perhaps the nation's only "nightscaper," visiting in Peoria, said he was "truly impressed with the tremendous native beauty in the topography here."

William J. Locklin, president of Loran, Inc., Redlands, Calif., was invited to Peoria by the Forest Park Foundation to attend a meeting Thursday night at which the Foundation told of progress made in improving the Peoria area riverfront and obtaining open space for future park and recreational development.

"One of our products is known as 'Nightscaping,'" Locklin said in an interview, describing this as "enhancing the beauty of existing architecture and landscaping at night."

The 45-year-old head of a national firm which manufactures garden lighting equipment said he developed "nightscaping" as a hobby 15 years ago and in the intervening years has seen it grow into an integral part of the firm of which he is

WILLIAM LOCKLIN

president.

Locklin said his firm is engaged in beautifying Williamsburg, Va., which he said is "probably second only to Washington, D.C. in importance as a tourist attraction on the Atlantic seaboard." He said the work at Williamsburg is being done in sections.

HE HAS BECOME nationally known for "nightscaping" various private and public garden sites and many types of buildings.

Locklin says he teaches contractors and architects the basic concept of outdoor illumination and that, then, his firm does the design work.

"The effect is to be seen and not the source," he said.

Loran, Inc., has distributors in 40 states for its garden lighting equipment.

Locklin travels extensively, and said that he found in Peoria — through the meeting at which he was an observer—"a remarkable spirit of togetherness." He recalled that Illinois Youth Commission Chairman John Troike had used that expression in remarks at the meeting.

Locklin was taken for a drive Thursday night, including a look-see at Glen Oak Park and said he was very impressed with the native beauty of that park and progress made in improving it.

He mentioned, specifically, the pavilion and the zoo and

said he would "hold both of these as beautiful examples of architecture."

On the other hand, he said he was "appalled to see the lack of nighttime beauty or even visibility." He added:

"When parks are lit up from within they are made so inviting that people will come to them. And everyone finds himself in true proportion to his fellow man, in a park."

Locklin's belief is that "beauty is contagious just as politeness is," and that once contractors and architects are given the basic ideas about nighttime outdoor illumination this is all that is necessary.

HE SAYS, also, that if properly illuminated parks will result in surrounding land values increasing immediately because the area becomes more desirable.

Locklin said he would like to work with some of the Peoria people "to get them motivated, to help them see the tremendous potential there is here."

Locklin is an electrical contractor and engineer in his native state of California.

Peoria, Illinois—one of the countless towns I visited, trying to drum up business

Oh, the ad came out beautifully. I'm sure a bundle of homeowners in places like Duluth, Minnesota and Tampa, Florida gazed at it longingly and sighed. The only problem? There was only one place in America where you could buy my fixtures: Redlands, California. Sure, all these people with relatives on the board could get me to fly out and install a system, but for the average Joe and Josephine in Des Moines, there just wasn't any availability.

Still, it wasn't too much later that the distribution picture improved. This was the very beginning of the 1960s, mind you, and things were done a little differently. We didn't have the Internet and whatnot to buy things from. If I'd started Nightscaping-Loran in 2006 the picture would have been quite different. At that time, however, it was one shot. Then the magazine is tossed out and you're left holding a huge bill.

There were still some bumps left before we really started getting distribution. One such situation involved an inquiry from a legitimate distributor in San Francisco. The inquiry was made by phone, not too long after the *House Beautiful* ad. I spoke to them twice on the phone and they seemed genuinely interested.

"Okay, then," I said. "I'll come up and show you my line."

So I drove up to San Francisco, which, as I remember, took most of one day. I arrived in a bewildering downtown full of hills bigger than I'd ever seen in any city. These people were located on Folsom street, I remembered. Right in the thick of things.

Well, I drove up and down those big hills for a while, maybe 30 minutes. Couldn't find a single place to park. Meanwhile I'm getting lost, going all over the place, and crawling straight up and down what seemed to be small mountains.

So I decide to turn right around and come home. Drove back to Redlands right that minute. Sixteen and more hours on the road, thirty minutes at my destination. *The great salesman in action.*

The funny thing? I know people who've had worse experiences with San Francisco. But this was a fantastic example of the kind of ineptitude I sometimes displayed as a young entrepreneur. Now I just have to look back and smile, thinking about how ridiculous I could be at times.

Another good example of the dangers of professional advice/conventional wisdom comes from my dealings with chain stores, which, suffice to say, have not been as fruitful as one might think. Of course anyone who comes up with a new product will generally think, "My goodness, Store X wants to carry my line?! I've made it!"

It's not quite that easy, though, in practice.

Let's go backward in time for a moment. A few years ago one of our Nightscaping contractors did an installation for a man associated with one of the "big-box" retail stores, as they're so affectionately known. In fact, the man was more than just associated. He was the chairman of the board.

The client was impressed with Nightscaping. He loved the effect, admired the quality of the equipment. In very short order he'd ordered his electrical buyer to contact us and initiate negotiations to begin carrying our line. Cue all the conventional wisdom: *of course you should do it! You'll make money hand over fist!*

Yet because of an experience with another national retailer—something I'll get to in a moment, which happened a ways back—I'm gun-shy when it comes to national chains. I've learned well that a lot of my strength, as a manufacturer, lies in the loyalty of our network, in our independent distributors and contractors.

So I quickly told the buyer I wasn't interested—a response he wasn't used to getting, I'm sure. He pressed me, however, insisting on a face-to-face meeting. Reluctantly I gave him an appointment for ten days down the line.

When the day came he walked into my office right on time. Our meeting lasted about 15 minutes. Not much changed.

"Sir," I said. "I am not interested. I will not sell to you."

The man was flabbergasted. I was sure by this point that he'd never received an answer like this. Especially from a small supplier like us. He didn't seem quite sure what to do. So he left.

Ten days later he called me back, however. Asked me for one more appointment. *Well, what do I have to lose? Nothing.*

"Sure, come on out, but I won't sell."

A few days later he showed up in my office again. Before he'd been in the room more than a minute, he opens up his briefcase, and with some fanfare pulls out a signed purchase order for one million dollars. Quite a payday.

I stared at it for a moment, counting all the zeros. Yup, a million. Lot of money for one order, and one thinks it wouldn't be the last. *Still. You know better.*

"Sir, I will not sell to you."

And that, finally, was that. The purchase order disappeared back into his briefcase, and I never saw the man again.

To many people this move would be well-nigh inexplicable. *Isn't the point, after all, to secure as wide a distribution for your product as possible?* Well, in a perfect world, yes. But not at the expense of quality. Not at the expense of customer service. And not at the expense of our wonderful independent distributors.

I'm proud to work with these small businesses, these loyal distributors who appreciate our style, the fact that after all these years our products are still made here in America. I'm proud to have remained independent; I like to work with like-minded people. It's "Friends Doing Business with Friends," after all.

Besides, once you accept one of those big checks from a big box, you'll begin to lose autonomy. Pretty soon you'll find yourself dancing to their tune. But I digress.

The reason I'm suspicious when it comes to national retailers is that I've gone there before. This gentleman from the big box wasn't first buyer coming around waving a check. Fifteen years before it, nearly the same thing had happened.

In this case it was the chairman of the board of Sears, Roebuck, Inc.

The man was vacationing in Hawaii and had seen some of our beautiful lighting installations there. Same story. He came back and told his electrical buyer that they needed this product. So I was contacted. The difference is, this time I said *yes.*

I was green, unsophisticated. I didn't know what that kind of big change could do to a business. And believe me, very few of my professional-advice givers saw this as anything but a no-brainer.

"Okay," I said. "Let's go."

The first thing I did was meet with their marketing people. We figured out a general plan, what direction we'd go in. Then I took the Sears purchase order, which had an unprecedented (for us) number of zeros on it, to the bank. I had no trouble securing a loan with that kind of back-up.

So we borrowed money and ramped up production. Began putting together the first 12-V do-it-yourself kits ever produced. They designed four different kits. We made the fixtures, paid for the paper inserts, the packaging, and all such things. It was a huge expense, but I was thrilled to be in Sears. You can't believe how thrilled. It was akin to a baseball player making the major leagues or an actor getting onto Broadway. A milestone.

Soon the first delivery was due. Proud as a new papa, I went down with a shipment to one of their major stores in LA. There I talked to the manager of the electrical department, instructing him in the ins and outs of our fixtures, the installation, etc. Things he needed to pass on to the customers. I spent a little while checking out the electrical department. Everything looked beautiful. Fantastic.

Well, I'm not sure I'd made it the 65 miles back to Redlands before we received a call from one of our Sears customers. They'd bought one of the kits, brought it home, installed it, plugged it in, and then immediately blew out every light in the set.

What was the problem? The salesman had forgotten to tell them they needed a transformer to step the voltage down from standard 120 to our safe 12. Whoops.

As it turned out, this was the least of our worries. Or maybe I should say the tip of the iceberg. The problem, I soon found, was in expertise. I'd take a delivery down to a California store, train the department manager in selling, and teaching about, Nightscaping products, and then before I turned around twice he'd be transferred, maybe to the paint department or ladies' ready-to-wear.

I couldn't keep up with training at all these stores, with their revolving doors. This led to a lot of problems. A lot of returns from unhappy customers who hadn't been informed about the product they were buying. You could almost hear the sounds of bulbs popping and circuits melting all over California.

Now, with all these deliveries, Sears had made few sales. Many of the kits they did sell had been returned. The bean counters in Chicago took a look at this and said, "Hmm. This isn't good." The line was discontinued.

Meanwhile, I had all these kits. Lots and lots. And nothing to do with them. Where they eventually ended up, that's another story. The moral here is that I ended up owing a lot of money to the bank due to this adventure. In fact, they were the only entity that benefited from my ill-advised foray into national retail. Of course, the bank never loses, I've noticed. No matter what happens, they always seem to get paid.

For the young entrepreneur, I reiterate, it's absolutely essential to make your own decisions—provided you've studied the market, know your business inside and out, etc. It should be your instincts, your knowledge, that provide direction for your company. To fail to take the reins, to twist and turn in the winds that will blow from a hundred directions—this is to risk losing control of all your hard work.

Your vision should be, if you're striking out on your own, singular. If you're always out of ideas, never know what to do next, it's a pretty good sign that you're not cut out for the entrepreneurial life. Not everyone is.

Luckily, for most people decision-making is a skill that can be honed. Indecisive people can learn to shed their hems-and-haws. Impulsive people can learn to be more judicious. And yes, sometimes stubborn people can learn to take the advice of others.

Concepts

- **Professional advice can be deadly to a new business.** Remember, every business has its own unique DNA. No two will have the same path to success. So it's important to make decisions for yourself, as even the most well-intentioned of sages can lead you astray.

- You'll come across loads of people with their own agendas; in fact, **everyone you meet in the business world will have their own agenda.** This is something to keep firmly in mind as you hear their "professional advice."

- Unless you **weigh the facts and figure out where you stand early**, it's very easy to get caught up in the opinions of others, which will often be contradictory and confusing.

- **Conventional wisdom can weigh your business down.** It's a new age, and the conventional wisdom, worn enough in its prime, in many cases simply does not fit anymore.

- **Check yourself at every stage of planning, during every decision-making process**, especially in the beginning. Try to identify whether you're doing things according to conventional wisdom or are truly weighing the needs of your business in today's climate, discarding everything useless and outmoded.

- **You must be a maverick to survive as an entrepreneur.** Few succeed, many will not. The difference often lies in the temperament of an individual.

- **Those who are terminally indecisive and dependent on the ideas of others** will generally not make particularly good entrepreneurs. Leadership is a crucial quality, as is vision. People who never seem to know what to do next usually don't inspire a great deal of confidence in their fellows.

- **Decision-making is a skill that can be honed.** If you focus on this aspect of your business life, examining how you come to decisions, what obstacles block you, and examine your decision-making process in relation to outcomes, it is possible to be more decisive, judicious, and open-minded.

10 Reflection Questions

1. Do you consider yourself a good decision-maker? Are you more likely to make decisions intuitively and impulsively, or to hem and haw for hours, days, weeks?

2. Think of the decisive people you've come across in your business or professional life. Can you identify any traits they have in common?

3. In your opinion, what combination of qualities make for an effective leader? Do you believe that someone in a leadership position should have to "earn" her authority? How?

4. Do you commonly play out important future scenarios in your mind? How adept are you at identifying crucial forks in the path ahead?

5. Are you easily influenced by others or do you tend to stick to your own decisions and conclusions?

6. Do you find yourself going "by the book" most of the time as a default mode, or do you approach each situation with new eyes, examining the particulars of each case?

7. Do you have trouble expressing your opinion to others, especially when it differs from theirs?

8. Do you tend to assume that people you come across in the business world automatically know more than you, are more savvy than you?

9. Are you proficient at listening to the advice of others in a neutral manner, storing it away for further thought? Do you tend to agree too quickly, or, on the other hand, dismiss others' ideas too quickly?

10. Do you tend to make decisions that favor results in the long term or short term? What do you believe is the proper balance between the two?

Chapter 10

Manage Fairly
(Groom Your Employees to Be Great)

My Story

My career has been blessed in a number of ways. Among the greatest of its blessings have been the wonderful people with whom I've had the privilege of being associated over the years. Many of these people have been, and are, employees of mine.

Good employees are a priceless resource

The motto "Friends Doing Business with Friends" has stuck with me for a long time, as I mentioned in a previous chapter. It's served me exceptionally well as a manager, too. It's not always easy being the boss. There are plenty of conflicts and issues to be dealt with. The fine art of managing other people is a tough lesson for many entrepreneurs to learn, and the inability to learn it sinks a great deal of them.

I think the most important thing—the first rule, I suppose—is to treat people who work for you as you would like to be treated. The golden rule is as effective in managerial relationships as it is in normal old human ones.

All too often there's an assumption of an adversarial relationship where there doesn't need to be. If you're fair with your pay and benefits, if you give your employees everything you can give them and are as open with them as possible, there should be no reason for the folks you hire to hold anything against you. If, on the other hand, you take the point of view that your employees are there to be cogs, to be manipulated and bullied into doing their jobs, to be compensated as meagerly as possible, to be disposed of summarily whenever it seems expedient—if you see them like this, they will respond in the same manner, and that adversarial relationship you created will indeed crop up, be strengthened, perpetuated, locked in stone.

I'm never understand the business owners or managers who insist on nickel-and-diming their employees, who push them beyond reasonable limits or ask the impossible. This is what's known as *penny wise, pound foolish*. Meaning that the little extra you squeeze out of your employees through low wages and higher productivity, you will lose through the millions of ways unhappy employees can hurt you. Who's more likely to be a thief or a hardcore loafer or even a saboteur—the happy, well-paid, appreciated employee or the terminally disgruntled, underpaid, overworked one?

Labor relations have changed a great deal over the past forty years. When I was coming up in the fifties, unions were strong. Management was expected in many cases to be the enemy, and the union was to be the mediator between two warring sides. No matter what your ideology, there's no way around the fact that the power of labor unions has declined a great deal. Most workers are not members, whereas when I was young a very sizable percentage were. In this climate, the responsibility for fairness falls on the employer. The hope here is that most business owners have evolved enough to see the benefits in having happy, secure workers. Sure the ethos is changing; when I was a young boy the relationship between employee and employer was most often considered one of natural enmity; now it seems a great number of people have realized that every business is a partnership and the more the employees feel invested in this partnership, the better they will perform. I point to the rise of profit-sharing schemes as a prime example of the new types of relationships emerging.

Let me say here that unions meant a great deal to me in my early career. I joined the International Brotherhood of Electrical Workers (IBEW) very early on, and being assured of a steady salary was extremely important in starting my business. The union membership was also key to my three years of travel around the United States, as I was able to stop at any union hall in any town and walk out with some kind of work.

I first learned something about unions and how they work at the cement plant in Colton. Shortly after I joined the IBEW, there was a strike meeting called. Being a kid, I went to the meeting to see what was going on. The owner of the cement plant was present at the meeting. When he was given a chance to speak, he began questioning key employees one at a time, asking each one about the condition of their department. And one by one they had to admit their silos and warehouses were full.

So the owner merely shrugged.

"As you can see," he said, "business isn't that good. When you fellas decide to go to work let me know."

Then he reached into his pocket and pulled a roll of bills from his pocket.

"I'm going to Palm Springs to rest. Again, when you're ready to go to work, let me know."

We never lost a day of work, in the end.

I always think it's best to keep your employees up on the condition of your business. Openness, to me, is a managerial virtue. They're also much more likely to understand their compensation or any problems you might have if they're fluent in the workings of the business. I believe this transparency, this opportunity to understand the workings of the business, should be extended to even the most entry-level, temporary employee. Every position.

Luis, a draftsman, creates a lighting plan

This is part of the education I would like every employee to have. To me, giving your employees the opportunity to learn, thrive, and move up is absolutely paramount. It's also important to make sure they're trained to the fullest extent possible for the job they're currently doing, of course. An employee can never have too much knowledge, too many skills.

The importance of this was drilled into me, as an owner and manager, from the beginning. I remember one particular instance not too long after getting set up in Redlands. At this point I was doing well as an independent contractor and was able to employee three men. Among my clients was a very fine commercial winery.

Well, one day the wine master called me up and said he had a problem with their major pump. It was about a two-hour drive to the winery, and I sent one of my best men to make the necessary repairs. Once he got there he went to work immediately, trying to trace out the problem. Now, this pump was only a small part of a multi-switch control system. Translation: this was a very complex thing to deal with, and isolating the problem could take any amount of time.

In any case, the mechanic I sent was standing there trying to trace out the wiring, see what was involved, and understand the system and its connections. The owner came down to watch him. After a few minutes, apparently unhappy with the slow pace of the repair, the owner instructed him to "cut a wire, do something."

Sure enough, my employee reaches right in and cuts a handful of wires. This was a tremendous mistake. He sees this immediately after doing it. So he holds the handful of cut wires out to the owner and says, "See, they're custom wires. Are you happy?"

Teaching at Nightscaping "University"

Actually, no one went home really happy that day. Needless to say, I lost this very good account. I wasn't happy with the employee, and he wasn't too pleased with himself. I suppose the aspect of education that would have been involved here is client relations. After that I really understood that teaching my employees, and learning myself, was an ongoing process and a vital one.

One of the nastier situations I've been involved with, in terms of business relations, occurred in Bergen, New Jersey. This was during my time traveling the States. I'd gotten a job at the Hackensack Evening Record. What a paranoid, awful environment. And it all started with the boss, the owner of the company, who paid all of us in cash rather than by check. According to him, this was his method of protesting all the taxes and insurance he was obligated by law to pay. Instead he gave it all to us in the form of play money. In this ugly place I found no one trusted one another, and the scene sickened me to my core. It didn't take long for us to decide to move on.

That was just about my worst experience with an employer. My worst experience *as* an employer came years later, when Nightscaping was still in its formative stages. After the *House Beautiful* ad debacle, where anyone seeing the ad would basically have had to hunt me out in Redlands, California, it soon became evident that if I ever wanted to get sales outside my backyard I needed a sales force. The natural way to go about this, in my opinion, was to begin developing a network of independent reps all around the country.

I did just that. Over the next ten years I began a routine of leaving my Redlands home on a Sunday, arriving in some distant location, meeting a rep, having dinner, and getting acquainted. Then, the next morning, we would call on area distributors, contractors, architects, and anyone who would listen. This usually took two days. After that I would either fly to some other distant location to start the process all over again, or fly home for a brief rest before leaving the next Sunday.

After ten years I had 30 independent reps covering the US and Canada. I was operating under the motto, "Friends Doing Business with Friends"—sharing it with all of them, then doing all I could to let them know I meant it. Well, right after I'd finished building this team, I soon learned that not everyone believed as strongly in my motto as I did.

As it turns out, my sales force had been courted secretly by a Fortune 500 company that was involved in the lighting business. They were all working independently, but there was communication going on between them. A core group was planning a mutiny; perhaps treason is a better word. This bunch walked "across the street" all together, and took all the contacts we'd developed with them.

I was shocked and felt betrayed. After all the time I'd spent developing these relationships, growing these salespeople, this is what I got? I didn't feel much better when I learned, a while later, that this had been what's called a "pump and dump" operation, wherein the company extracts all the useful information they can from these individuals, then lets them go. I don't remember if I gave a bitter laugh or not. Except for the underhanded company, no one came out ahead in that mess.

All I could do, at that point, was put my head down and rebuild. I did just that, reorganizing the sales force and developing what I have today—a better and more loyal team. Today, I have a fantastic national group, as well as an incredible bunch here in Redlands. Several of my employees have been with me between 20 and 25 years. Everything I am today, all my success, I owe to these people, individually and collectively. This also goes for people I employed earlier who have since left.

My vice president/general manager in particular has been an irreplaceable piece of the puzzle. Twenty-five years ago he came to me, having just earned his master's degree in business administration. He applied for the position of controller. We did an interview over the phone, and in my ignorance the only question I could ask was, "What the hell is controller?"

"I'll control your finances," he answered.

"Great," I said, laughing. "I don't have any. Lots of luck. You're hired."

What orders did I give him 25 years ago when he first showed up for work? I said he had to have more cash every Friday night than he did on the previous Monday morning. It didn't matter how much. Just more.

For 25 years he's never failed me in this—the margin's been as slim as five cents, but he's never once missed his mark. How can you put a price tag on that kind of employee? You can't. You just give them all you can and hope it's enough to make them happy. My goal is to make all my employees that good at what they do, that indispensable.

Be Remarkable... Get out of your rut !

One of the many motivational signs we keep up

This simple rule, this cash-on-hand form of business and financial management has worked well for me over the years, and I would recommend it to anyone venturing into business. I would recommend it to anyone simply trying to balance their household finances and save for the future. And I would certainly recommend it to the federal government.

But that's another story, perhaps another debate, and it surely doesn't belong here—in what's been both a modest seminar and the recounting of a life in business. My only hope is that it's been helpful, that someone young and dreaming will be aided by it, perhaps using it as a shred of a map, a light, something that can help them, in the dark, identify both the dangerous curves and potholes, and the wide, beautiful roads that lead to success.

And it is with this wish that I say thank you for listening, and I close up the dusty book of my life, leaving the rest untold. With a modest bow, appropriate for the small accomplishments I've had (in relation to the great ones had by others), I leave the stage.

Concepts

- **Managing your employees fairly** is one of the most important things you can do to keep your business alive and well.

- An **unharmonious workplace will be a drag on any new enterprise**, able to sink even the worthiest of new companies.

- It's impossible to put a price tag on the **contributions of happy, well-compensated, loyal, and effective employees**. As a corollary, it's impossible to accurately asses the dollar amount you'll lose by alienating your employees, which will result in a dramatic increase in the worst workplace practices.

- **Managers and owners can either reinforce or undermine the assumptions of an adversarial relationship between themselves and their employees.** Being as fair as you know how to be goes a long way toward undermining them.

- **"Squeezing" your employees is a penny-wise, pound-foolish enterprise** as it poisons relations and destroys the team—and partnership-oriented mindset it's so important to develop in your company.

- In an age where the power and reach of unions has tended to, and probably will continue to, diminish, **it's largely becoming up to the employer to pick up the slack and look out for the concerns of his employees.**

- **Developing a solid team** is a type of investment, involving much time, money, and effort, and you should view it as such.

- **Educating your employees is a perpetual process**, and you should be yourself all the time learning in order to ensure you have the ability to pass on knowledge.

10 Reflection Questions

1. Have you ever managed anyone? If yes, what are the most immediate lessons you remember from the experience?

2. When put in positions of leadership, do you tend to consider your own self-interest or the interests of the group as a whole. What do you believe to be the proper balance?

3. What do you believe the employer's responsibility to his employees to be? Should he be responsible for their financial well-being? Their health care? Their retirement? Or do his true obligations end when he pays the agreed amount each week?

4. How good are you at conflict management and resolution? How would you, in a general sense, go about addressing disagreements between employees?

5. What is your opinion of unions? How much do you know about their workings? Do you know anyone with union membership?

6. What are, in your opinion, the most efficient methods for building company loyalty?

7. How do you feel about mechanisms such as profit-sharing? How much should workers share in the fortunes of the company?

8. Who are your role models when it comes to management? What traits do they have in common?

9. To what extent should an employer try to be friends with his employees? Is there, in your opinion, a danger in an overly friendly relationship?

10. Have you ever fired someone? What situations, in your opinion, demand termination? Should the circumstances of a worker's home and financial life have any bearing on the decision?

The 10 Most Important Reminders

1. There is **no magic formula** that assures a person of success in business or life. Determination is probably the biggest indicator of who will prevail in their entrepreneurship. *Believe in yourself.*

2. **Creativity is a basic requirement** for anyone who'd like to build a business from the ground up. If you're not someone who likes to invent, figure out new ways to do things, or improvise around traditional themes, you might want to rethink your future ambitions. *Be resourceful . . . and persistent.*

3. Becoming an independent entrepreneur is hard work, sometimes backbreaking, and the **long hours and extreme dedication required can stretch on for years.** Thus if you're not truly interested in what you're doing, your chances of holding on through the hard times will be severely diminished. *Follow your instincts . . . and interests.*

4. Without an expansion of your knowledge base, your business will founder. **A good idea to start with isn't enough.** You must consistently learn, both to keep ahead of any competition and to satisfy the market you're trying to serve. *Search for knowledge.*

5. **The ability to envision the future** is *the* key trait of a successful entrepreneur and the common denominator of those who achieve the most. *Success is mañana.*

6. **Invest the relatively small amount of time necessary to nurture your business relationships.** They will often pay you back many times over. (And it's worth it to remember real friendships can be fun and rewarding outside the sphere of business as well.) *Make friends . . . a lot of friends.*

7. Even if you're not that interested in local involvement, you should still try for **some level of effective representation**, for exposure and networking purposes if nothing else. (Community involvement and civic life can be addicting, however, so don't be surprised to see yourself going from apathetic to hooked.) *Get involved with your local (and non-local) communities.*

8. It's easy to get lost in the vagaries of business-school formulas or product specifications, but in the end, it all comes down to one thing: **is the client/customer happy or not?** *Understand your customers' motivations.*

9. **Those who are terminally indecisive and dependent on the ideas of other** will generally not make particularly good entrepreneurs. Leadership is a crucial quality, as is vision. People who never seem to know what to do next usually don't inspire a great deal of confidence in their fellows. *Watch out for professional advice (and conventional wisdom).*

10. It's impossible to put a price tag on the **contributions of happy, well-compensated, loyal, and effective employees**. As a corollary, it's impossible to accurately asses the dollar amount you'll lose by alienating your employees, which will result in a dramatic increase in the worst workplace practices. *Manage fairly (groom your employees to be great).*

Friends Doing Business with Friends

A little while ago, as this book was being written, I sent out a request through my NIGHTchat system, an email forum that connects our many contractors. Asking for advice on the most important thing an aspiring entrepreneur should know, I received some excellent replies, and would like to share them with you here, in their original form. My thanks go out to all the folks who contributed, and who continue to make Nightscaping® a vibrant and wonderful place to be a part of.

* * *

Bill,

In answer to your question: The most important step, story, or action that a new entrepreneur needs to know is: (this is of course off the top of my head and could easily change in the next min, hour, day, week) Find or Create and then Fill a NICHE! It is easy to say but getting harder and harder to do. None the less, I think that if a new upstart wants to move along successfully they need to find a hole in the marketplace and then develop their product/service to fill that void. I don't care if you are going to be a painter, lighting contractor, plumber, web developer, graphic artist or retailer . . . . you have to find a niche. If the market seems flooded but you have all the passion in the world to be a house painter, then find a new product that you can use that no one else offers. Add service to your product mix. Do something, anything that makes you stand out from the crowd and offers the marketplace an alternative that was not previously available.

—**James Solecki,** *Ontario, Canada*

William "Bill" Locklin

Bill,

    Find your passion and figure out a way to make money doing it
    Pilot your ideas with someone you trust
    Document your critical processes so that they are teachable
    Write down your business plan
    Adequately capitalize at the start-up
    Give at least 10% of all your gross profit to a charity that's investing in the encouragement and building up of people . . . . be a giver
    Invest back into your business
    Pursue excellence
    Develop your workers
    Grow profitably
    Replicate yourself
    Increase your understanding of your product or service
    Carefully listen to your customers
    Get your ideas to market faster
    Make yourself and your business accountable to someone of excellent character
    Don't believe the good things people are saying about you
    Give credit to the Lord who made you . . . for all your ability

—**Michael Murray,** *New Jersey*

Bill,

    As a business owner I feel like the single most important characteristic is perseverance. You will be out of money, energy, will power, enthusiasm, and ideas but when you keep on keeping on all these things will reappear. Perseverance, that's the key.

—**Bob Cooper, *NORTH CAROLINA***

Bill,

    How? . . . "Passion."

    You take a hundred guys . . . or a thousand . . . or ten thousand. They're all doing the same thing. What makes one guy stand out? What makes one guy create something new? Something special? Something remarkable? It's his (or her) "passion."

    When you walked your first property in the late '50s to assist an existing client on his personal residence, were you thinking, "Gee . . . I think I'll start a company. Maybe all my products will be low-voltage. Maybe I'll call it *Nightscaping*. Maybe I'll create a whole new industry? [No.] I'm guessing it was your passion that brought you to where you are today.

You still have it and you have shared it. I have four children and three grandchildren. Put me down for eight "signed copies" of that book (the extra one is for me).

—**Jeff Vinachi,** *Florida*

Friend,

It's about time you got started! I'll tell you what I want to read in a book by Bill Locklin. An autobiography! Tell me about your life from your earliest memories till now. Tell me what you learned from all the experiences. Tell me where your strength and tenacity come from. What experiences caused you to be an exceptional human among humans. Why do you still have more drive in you than the vast majority of our fellows on the planet? I don't want to read another business book, there are millions of them already. I want Bill Locklin, uncut and uncensored. Can I get an amen!

—**Kevin Islander,** *California*

Bill,

Well I've spent a couple days now thinking about your request and I still can't say I have anything for you. So, I'll just say the thoughts that I have out loud and see what comes about.

I kind of 'stumbled' into owning a business so I don't feel qualified or justified in saying to someone, "Do what I did."

Looking back however, after 33 years of business, I would say to a newcomer: "Look for a product/service mix that you feel passion for. You may be living with it for quite a while."

Choose your business associates (employees/partners/consultants) with the same scrutiny that you would pick a spouse/lifelong friend; they're going to be your 'other' family.

Be very honest with yourself on your personal history. How well have you stuck to the 'game,' especially when the game got difficult or boring. Past performance is usually a pretty good predictor of future and a failed business can be quite expensive financially and personally.

Playing off your words, Bill, I'd suggest the newcomer ask, "How good have I been at keeping my promises?" The ultimate reputation of the business falls on the shoulders of the owner.

Do you have an open and hungry mind? Adaptation and innovation are essential to the survival/success of a business. If you're doing it just for the money, stop and reconsider. The money isn't always that much better than working as a highly qualified technician/manager of a proven firm and the burden of responsibility and risk can be far less working for someone else.

Do you like surprises? Even nasty ones? Well, they're likely to happen! (Remember those rusty fixtures? Yikes! ;))

Are you ok with being alone? There are likely to be a number of occasions when that's how it feels.

The prior question brings up maybe the most important issue for me. Spiritual grounding. If you think you're the 'doer' of it all you're in for a rough ride.

—

Now Bill,

About your book. I know this is not going to be one more of those "How to succeed in business" books filled with platitudes that have already been inscribed in oh so many tomes of business wisdom. I'm looking forward to reading the honest, right from the heart, loving and gritty tale of one cocky, foolish, crazy and just plain Bill Locklin. I anticipate being regaled about submarines, marriage, raising a family, oranges, horses, faith, juice cans, major successes, major failures, lessons learned, people loved, troubled times, heroes and villains, births, deaths, and, well . . . the whole nine yards. I'm looking forward to a good cry or two, more than a few good laughs and numerous hallelujahs.

Not expecting much, just the truth, straight from the soul and experiences of one Bill Locklin.

And Bill, there's a spot on my 'must read' list waiting anxiously for your book. So, get cracking!

With love,
—Mike Islander, *California*

Bill,

I think one of the most important traits of a successful business is perseverance. Some times I feel like a salmon swimming up stream. You have to keep paddling to get to that next "pond"!

—John Saul, *Kansas*

Bill,

When I started my own business I felt that I could never again complain about anything that affected my income, my personal time, or my concept of a quality job well done. When I first started I feel the most important things that kept me afloat and prosperous was a willingness to do "whatever it takes," whether it be 23-hour days, working in the rain, promising things that were near impossible to deliver and delivering etc . . . I also feel that a healthy dose of fear was good at the time as well. Not fear of being on my own but rather fear about making the mortgage payment, putting groceries on the table, and not being a failure to my family. Lastly as many others have echoed I feel that business ethics grounded in faith was the foundation upon which the business was built. 30 years after the fact I still have people tell me they remember this quality about our company and its employees. Good luck. Have FUN. Warmest

—Rob DiSchino, *MASS*

Bill,

We're expected to tell you how to run a successful business?? I completely agree with Bob, Jeff, Steve and Rob. After seeing a lot of business' some good and some not so good here is what I'd say. First of all you have to be a exceptional leader that is well organized and that can motivate people. You have to be tough, committed, loyal, hardworking, full of integrity, competitive attitude, someone who never stops learning and a man of faith. You ALWAYS must treat others the way you want to be treated. Lastly I would say you must be able to turn off work and spend quality family time at the end of the work day. Looking forward to reading your book!

—Tim McKay, *COLORADO*

Bill,

"Stay Focused on Today"—I have a simple habit to stay focused that has taught me many valuable lessons and continues to serve me today. It's almost become a ritual, the same way certain athletes have them with game day procedures like lucky socks or red shirts on Sunday, or eating chicken before every game. But, my "ritual" is easy to put into action and is my basic strategy for being prepared. After starting my lighting business at 39, I became more focused than in my whole prior life. I had to. There were many quiet nights at the dinner table when all you heard was silverware clinking the plate. And, Joyce would ask, "Did you sell anything today? No honey, but I'm close."

Just as I walk into a meeting, appointment or presentation; I pause for a moment and ask myself what is it that I want to leave the meeting, appointment or presentation feeling as if I have achieved? The physical act of verbalizing what I want helps me stay focused on getting it. I would think that someone starting a new business might also find this to be an effective strategy.

It's not foolproof. There are times when I have skipped the prep and would "wing it", because I felt I couldn't afford the extra time it would take to assess what it was that I wanted to leave feeling as if I achieved. But the truth is that I'm always more effective when I take the time, prior to any business face-to-face, to assess what I want to achieve, and actually, it saves time. "Winging it" was false economy for me, and a time bandit, because being unfocused makes a meeting last longer, and the follow up longer and much harder to do.

Bill, I hope my Business 101 tip helps. It's not flashy, or the most high tech. It's just simple ritual that helps me stay focused on one plate, when I feel like I have a lot of them spinning.

—**Doug Alderman, Florida**

Bill,

Good luck with the book project, I am enjoying the response to your announcement and request that we share some of our experiences.

There are many details of success, but for me the most important element, by far, has been the people I work with. I try not to complicate things, I am not a "business" man. I am a contractor who started a business 18 years ago. I have been self employed in the same business and had employees ever since. I went to college but did not study business. I worked my way through school in construction which I have always loved and I have always preferred to work in the trades. I stopped growing the size of my crew six years ago with twelve employees and began focusing on improving efficiency and the bottom line while increasing prices, wages and benefits. We have not had a single change in personnel in five years and some have been on as long as nine years. My crews are very experienced and efficient and every year it gets better. You cannot achieve that with workers coming and going. The result has been that we are one of the most sought after landscape design build and arbor care companies in our area. I have a job to do as owner and operations manager of the business and that starts with who I say good morning to six days a week. Safeguarding the morale of the company is probably what I consider the single most important thing I do. Without them all the signed contracts are worthless.

Starting a business and getting customers was simple, nothing fancy required, advertise, return phone calls, follow through, work, work, work, etc. Take risks to grow and learn and finish every job you start even if you take a loss. (Be sure to learn from those!) Stay out of debt, live below your means, focus on customer service and invest in the people you work with.

Naturally it is good to get involved in charity, it seems that most business owners understand this. I prefer to do so at a local level, because of the nature of our business we have the opportunity to give services to charitable projects around town and that is far more satisfying and engaging than writing checks, but no matter, whatever you give, that comes after you are established as with so many many aspects of running a business. Bill is the one writing the book, I just wanted to emphasize what is near and dear to my heart.

Buy lunch and eat at the jobsite often, that is the key to success :)
—**Scott LaPlante,** *California*

Printed in the United States
71239LV00004B/358-465